Knowledge: A Very Short Introduction

VERY SHORT INTRODUCTIONS are for anyone wanting a stimulating and accessible way into a new subject. They are written by experts, and have been translated into more than 45 different languages.

The series began in 1995, and now covers a wide variety of topics in every discipline. The VSI library now contains over 500 volumes—a Very Short Introduction to everything from Psychology and Philosophy of Science to American History and Relativity—and continues to grow in every subject area.

Titles in the series include the following:

Jennifer Nagel

KNOWLEDGE

A Very Short Introduction

OXFORD
UNIVERSITY PRESS

Great Clarendon Street, Oxford, OX2 6DP,
United Kingdom

Oxford University Press is a department of the University of Oxford.
It furthers the University's objective of excellence in research, scholarship,
and education by publishing worldwide. Oxford is a registered trade mark of
Oxford University Press in the UK and in certain other countries

© Jennifer Nagel 2014

The moral rights of the author have been asserted

First edition published in 2014

Published in the United States of America by Oxford University Press
198 Madison Avenue, New York, NY 10016, United States of America

British Library Cataloguing in Publication Data
Data available

Library of Congress Control Number: 2014937970

ISBN 978-0-19-966126-8

Printed and bound by
CPI Group (UK) Ltd, Croydon, CR0 4YY

Contents

Acknowledgements

For helpful comments and discussion I am grateful to Elena Derksen, Emma Ma, Alex Tenenbaum, Sergio Tenenbaum, and Tim Williamson. I am also grateful to the Social Sciences and Humanities Research Council of Canada for their support.

List of illustrations

Chapter 1
Introduction

Searching for knowledge

The hunt for knowledge has never been easier. Hard questions can
be answered with a few keystrokes. Our individual powers of
memory, perception, and reasoning can be double-checked by
distant friends and experts, with minimal effort. Past generations
would marvel at the number of books within our reach.

These new advantages don't always protect us from an old
problem: if knowledge is easy to get, so is mere opinion, and it can
be hard to spot the difference. A website that looks trustworthy
can be biased, world-renowned authorities can follow misleading
evidence down the wrong track, and illusions can distort what we
ourselves seem to see or remember. What at first seemed like
knowledge can turn out to be something less than the real thing.
Reflecting on the difficulty of enquiry, we can find ourselves
wondering exactly what this real thing might be. What is
knowledge? What is the difference between just thinking that
something is true and actually knowing that it is? How are we able
to know anything at all?

These questions are ancient ones, and the branch of philosophy
dedicated to answering them—epistemology—has been active for
thousands of years. Some core questions have remained constant

throughout this time: How does knowledge relate to truth? Do senses like vision and hearing supply us with knowledge in the same way as abstract reasoning does? Do you need to be able to justify a claim in order to count as knowing it? Other concerns have emerged only recently, in light of new discoveries about humanity, language, and the mind. Is the contrast between knowledge and mere opinion universal to all cultures? In ordinary language, does the word 'know' always stand for the same thing, or does it refer to something heavier in a court of law, and something lighter in a casual bus-stop conversation? What natural instinctive impressions do we have about what others know, and how much can these impressions tell us about knowledge itself?

Over the centuries, philosophers investigating knowledge have unearthed some strange puzzles and paradoxes. Philosophers have also developed some innovative solutions to these problems. After looking back at major historical developments in the theory of knowledge, this book presses forward into its central current debates. We begin with a tour of some features of knowledge that easily spark philosophical curiosity.

Knowledge and the knower

Knowledge is sometimes portrayed as a free-flowing impersonal resource: knowledge is said to be stored in databases and libraries, and exchanged through 'the knowledge economy', as information-driven commerce is sometimes called. Like many resources, knowledge can be acquired, used for diverse purposes, and lost—sometimes at great expense. But knowledge has a closer connection to us than resources like water or gold. Gold would continue to exist even if sentient life were wiped out in a catastrophe; the continued existence of knowledge, on the other hand, depends on the existence of someone who knows.

It's tempting to identify knowledge with facts, but not every fact is an item of knowledge. Imagine shaking a sealed cardboard box containing a single coin. As you put the box down, the coin inside the box has landed either heads or tails: let's say that's a fact. But as long as no one looks into the box, this fact remains unknown; it is not yet within the realm of knowledge. Nor do facts become knowledge simply by being written down. If you write the sentence 'The coin has landed heads' on one slip of paper and 'The coin has landed tails' on another, then you will have written down a fact on one of the slips, but you still won't have gained knowledge of the outcome of the coin toss. Knowledge demands some kind of access to a fact on the part of some living subject. Without a mind to access it, whatever is stored in libraries and databases won't be knowledge, but just ink marks and electronic traces. In any given case of knowledge, this access may or may not be unique to an individual: the same fact may be known by one person and not by others. Common knowledge might be shared by many people, but there is no knowledge that dangles unattached to any subject. Unlike water or gold, knowledge always belongs to someone.

More precisely, we should say that knowledge always belongs to some individual or group: the knowledge of a group may go beyond the knowledge of its individual members. There are times when a group counts as knowing a fact just because this fact is known to every member of the group ('The orchestra knows that the concert starts at 8 pm'). But we can also say that the orchestra knows how to play Beethoven's entire Ninth Symphony, even if individual members know just their own parts. Or we can say that a rogue nation knows how to launch a nuclear missile even if there is no single individual of that nation who knows even half of what is needed to manage the launch. Groups can combine the knowledge of their members in remarkably productive (or destructive) ways.

Is there knowledge beyond the knowledge of human individuals and groups? What should we say about what is known by non-human animals? Or by God, if there is a God? These questions

3

1. **Everything known must be linked to a knower**

threaten to pull us into difficult biological and theological debates. For this reason, most epistemologists start with the simpler case of the knowledge of a single human being (such as yourself). This kind of knowledge will be the main focus of this book. Knowledge, in the sense that matters here, is a link between a person and a fact. It remains challenging to describe this link, even when we restrict our attention to one knowing person and one known fact. What is it for you to know something, rather than merely believe it?

4

Spotting the difference

As soon as we ask about the difference between knowing something and just believing it, we might wonder how we can be so confident that there really *is* a difference. Consider the view that there is no real difference between knowledge and opinion. What if 'knowledge' is nothing more than a label we apply to the attitudes of the elite? In our culture, perhaps a Nobel Laureate's scientific research or a CEO's thoughts about his industry; in other times and places, the teachings of the high priest or the tribal elders. Across the board, the thoughts of underdogs get brushed off as superstitions and misconceptions. On this view—call it the Cynical Theory—whether someone's idea counts as knowledge or mere opinion would be determined by his status as a leader or a loser, and not by anything in the idea itself or its relation to reality.

It's not entirely crazy to think of knowledge as a status marker. It's surely right that 'knowledge' is an attractive label; to describe an attitude as knowledge is to rank it above many other attitudes. It is also plausible that there are strong links running both ways between knowledge and power: power typically delivers advantages that can help a person gain knowledge, and knowledge can often help a person gain power. It may even be true that our judgements about knowledge are often biased by the social standing of those we are evaluating. But the Cynical Theory says something more than that power and knowledge often go together, or are widely thought to go together: it says that there is nothing more to knowledge than the perception of power.

As a theory about how we actually use the term 'knowledge', the Cynical Theory fails to capture some relevant facts. It underestimates our ability to resist the ideas of the powerful: even winners of the Nobel Prize can be doubted and challenged. More generally, even if we are more likely to see the powerful as knowing, we can still recognize a distinction between knowing and just seeming to know: we are all aware of cases in which

5

experts once widely thought to know something have been proven wrong. The Cynical Theory also misses something notable about the way we talk about knowledge in everyday life. The verb 'to know' is not reserved for our descriptions of top experts and leaders: it's one of the ten most common verbs in English. It's the default verb for describing what happens as a result of ordinary cases of seeing, hearing, and remembering things: you know what you had for dinner last night, who won the last US presidential election, and whether you are now wearing shoes.

English is not unusual: across a vast array of languages—Russian, Mandarin, Welsh, Spanish—a word meaning 'know' is among the most common verbs. English does have one confusing feature, shared with a number of other languages: our verb 'know' has two distinct senses in common use. In the first, it can take either a propositional complement or 'that'-clause (as in 'He knows that the car was stolen') or an embedded question (as in 'She knows who stole the car' or 'She knows when the theft occurred'). In the second, it takes a direct object ('He knows Barack Obama'; 'She knows London'). Many other languages use different words for these two meanings (like the French 'savoir' and 'connaître'). In what follows, we will be focusing on the first sense of 'knows', the kind of knowledge that links a person with a fact.

This sense of 'knows' has an interesting feature: there's a word for it in all of the world's 6,000+ human languages ('think' shares this feature). This status is surprisingly rare: an educated person has a vocabulary of about 20,000 words, but fewer than 100 of these are thought to have precise translations in every other language. Common words you might expect to find in every language (like 'eat' and 'drink') don't always have equivalents. (Some aboriginal languages in Australia and Papua New Guinea get by with a single word meaning 'ingest'.) Elsewhere, other languages make finer rather than rougher distinctions: many languages lack a single word translating 'go', because they use distinct verbs for self-propelled motions like walking and for vehicular motion. Sometimes the lines

Box 1 Words that do and do not appear in all languages

Universal	Not universal
know, think, see, want, hear, say	eat, drink, stop, hit, go, sit
I, you	she, he, they
good, bad	happy, sad
not, maybe, because, if, true, before, after	plant, tree, animal, bird, cold, hot

are just drawn in different places: where the common English pronouns 'he' and 'she' force a choice of gender, other languages have third-person pronouns that distinguish between present and absent persons, but not between male and female. Human languages have remarkable diversity. But despite this diversity, a few terms appear in all known languages, perhaps because their meanings are crucial to the way language works, or because they express some vital aspect of human experience. These universals include 'because', 'if', 'good', 'bad', 'live', 'die'... and 'know' (see Box 1).

Knowing vs thinking

What do we ordinarily do with this vital verb, and how is 'know' different from the contrasting verb 'think'? Everyday usage provides some clues. Consider the following two sentences:

Jill knows that her door is locked.
Bill thinks that his door is locked.

We immediately register a difference between Jill and Bill—but what is it? One factor that comes to mind has to do with the truth of the embedded claim about the door. If Bill just thinks that his door is locked, perhaps this is because Bill's door is not really locked. Maybe he didn't turn the key far enough this morning as he was leaving home. Jill's door, however, must be locked for the sentence about her to be true: you can't ordinarily say, 'Jill knows that her door is locked, but her door isn't locked.' Knowledge links a subject to a truth. This feature of 'knowing that' is called *factivity*: we can know only facts, or true propositions. 'To know that' is not the only factive construction: others include 'to realize that', 'to see that', 'to remember that', 'to prove that'. You can realize that your lottery ticket has won only if it really has won. One of the special features of 'know' is that it is the most general such verb, standing for the deeper state that remembering, realizing, and the rest all have in common. Seeing that the barn is on fire or proving that there is no greatest prime number are just two of the many ways of achieving knowledge.

Of course, it's possible to *seem* to know something that later turns out to be false—but as soon as we recognize the falsity, we have to retract the claim that it was ever known. ('We thought he knew that, but it turned out he was wrong and didn't know.') To complicate matters, it can be hard to tell whether someone knows something or just seems to know it. This doesn't erase the distinction between knowing and seeming to know. In a market flooded with imitations it can be hard to tell a real diamond from a fake, but the practical difficulty of identifying the genuine article shouldn't make us think there is no difference out there: real diamonds have a special essence—a special structure of carbon atoms—not shared by lookalikes.

The dedicated link to truth is part of the essence of knowledge. We speak of 'knowing' falsehoods when we are speaking in a non-literal way (just as we can use a word like 'delicious' sarcastically, describing things that taste awful). Emphasis—in italics or pitch—is one sign of non-literal use. 'That cabbage soup smells *delicious*, right?' 'I *knew* I had been picked for the team.

But it turned out I wasn't.' This use of 'knows' has been called the 'projected' use: the speaker is projecting herself into a past frame of mind, recalling a moment when it seemed to her that she knew. The emphasis is a clue that the speaker is distancing herself from that frame of mind: she didn't literally or really know (as our emphatic speaker didn't really like the soup). The literal use of 'know' can't mix with falsehood in this way.

By contrast, belief can easily link a subject to a false proposition: it's perfectly acceptable to say, 'Bill thinks that his door is locked, but it isn't.' The verb 'think' is *non-factive*. (Other non-factive verbs include 'hope', 'suspect', 'doubt', and 'say'—you can certainly say that your door is locked when it isn't.) Opinions being non-factive does not mean that opinion is always wrong: when Bill just thinks that his door is locked, he could be right. Perhaps Bill's somewhat unreliable room-mate Bob occasionally forgets to lock the door. If Bill isn't entirely sure that his door is locked, then he could think that it is locked, and be right, but fail to know that it is locked. Confidence matters to knowledge.

Knowledge has still further requirements, beyond truth and confidence. Someone who is very confident but for the wrong reasons would also fail to have knowledge. A father whose daughter is charged with a crime might feel utterly certain that she is innocent. But if his confidence has a basis in emotion rather than evidence (suppose he's deliberately avoiding looking at any facts about the case), then even if he is right that his daughter is innocent, he may not really know that she is. But if a confidently held true belief is not enough for knowledge, what more needs to be added? This question turns out to be surprisingly difficult—indeed, difficult enough to warrant a whole chapter of its own (Chapter 4).

Because truth is such an important feature in the essence of knowledge, something further should be said about it here. We'll assume in what follows that truth is objective, or based in

9

reality and the same for all of us. Most philosophers agree about the objectivity of truth, but there are some rebels who have thought otherwise. The Ancient Greek philosopher Protagoras (5th century BCE) held that knowledge is always of the true, but also that different things could be true for different people. Standing outdoors on a breezy summer day and feeling a bit sick, I could know that the wind is cold, while you know that it is warm. Protagoras didn't just mean that I know that the wind feels cold to me, while you know that it feels warm to you—the notion that different people have different feelings is something that can be embraced by advocates of the mainstream view according to which truth is the same for everyone. (It could be a plain objective fact that the warm wind feels cold to a sick person.) Protagoras says something more radical: it is true for me that the wind really *is* cold and true for you that the wind *is* warm. In fact, Protagoras always understands truth as relative to a subject: some things are true-for-you; other things are true-for-your-best-friend or true-for-your-worst-enemy, but nothing is simply *true*.

Protagoras's relativist theory of knowledge is intriguing, but hard to swallow, and perhaps even self-refuting. If things really are for each person as he sees them, then no one ever makes a mistake. It's true for the hallucinating desert traveller that there really is an oasis ahead; it's true for the person who makes an arithmetical error that seven and five add up to eleven. What if it later seems to you that you have made a mistake? If things always are as they appear, then it is true for you that you have made a mistake, even though appearances can never be misleading, so it should have been impossible for you to get things wrong in the first place. This is awkward. One Ancient Greek tactic for handling this problem involved a division of you-at-this-moment from you-a-moment-ago. Things are actually only true for you-right-now, and different things might be true-for-you-later (for example, it might be true-for-your-future-self that your past self made a mistake).

Splintering the self into momentary fragments is arguably a high price to pay for a theory of knowledge. If you find the price too high, and want to hold on to the idea that there is a lasting self, then Protagoras's theory may start to seem false to you. But if Protagoras's theory seems false, remember that by the lights of this theory you can't be mistaken: the theory itself tells you that things always are for you as they seem to you. Now Protagoras's theory is really in trouble. The self-destructive potential of relativism was remarked upon by Plato (c.428–348 BCE), who also noticed a tension between what Protagoras was trying to do in the general formulation of his theory, and what the theory says about truth being local to the individual. If Protagoras wants his theory of what is true-for-each-person-at-an-instant to capture what is going on with all of us, over time, it's not clear how he can manage that.

Relative truth has had more sophisticated defenders since Protagoras, but most philosophers have favoured objective truth. What is true is true for all of us, full stop, whether or not we are aware of it. If we have to put it in terms of perspective, what is true is what would be the case from a God's-eye perspective. But is objective truth humanly knowable? Sceptics have raised some doubts about this.

Chapter 2
Scepticism

Can you be sure?

Think of one of the most trivial and easily checked facts you know.
For example, you know whether you are presently wearing
shoes. Right?

The sceptic would like you to reconsider. Could you be dreaming
that you are reading this book right now? If this is a dream, you
could be lying barefoot in bed. Or you could be asleep on the
commuter train, fully dressed. You may consider it unlikely that you
are now dreaming, but you might wonder whether you have any
way of establishing conclusively that you are awake, and that things
are as they seem. Perhaps you remember reading somewhere that
pinching yourself can end a dream—but did you read that in a
trustworthy source? Or is it even something that you *really* read, as
opposed to something that you are just now dreaming you once
read? If you can't find any sure way of proving that you are now
awake, can you really take your sensory experience at face value?

When you start to get self-conscious about what you know, even
the simplest fact, something you usually think you could verify at
a glance, can start to seem like something you don't really know.
Evidence that you would usually take for granted suddenly seems
dubious, and you may start to feel that certainty is slipping out of

2. What do you know?

reach, across the board. This pattern of thoughts has worried many philosophers over the centuries, deeply enough to drive some to doubt that human beings can have any substantive knowledge at all. These philosophers are 'sceptics', from the Ancient Greek for 'inquiring' or 'reflective'.

The historical roots of scepticism

Ancient Greece was in fact the birthplace of two distinct sceptical traditions, the Academic and the Pyrrhonian. Academic sceptics argued for the conclusion that knowledge was impossible; Pyrrhonian sceptics aimed to reach no conclusions at all, suspending judgement on all questions, even the question of the possibility of knowledge.

Academic Scepticism is named for the institution it sprang from: the Academy in Athens, originally founded by Plato. The movement's two great leaders each served a turn as head of the Academy: Arcesilaus in the 3rd century BCE, and then Carneades a hundred years later. Although both of them originally framed their scepticism in opposition to the once-influential Stoic theory of knowledge, their arguments continue to be taken seriously in philosophy to the present day. These sceptical arguments have enduring power because the core Stoic ideas they criticize are still embraced within many other theories of knowledge, and may even be part of our common-sense way of thinking about the difference between knowledge and mere belief.

Stoic epistemology draws a distinction between impressions and judgements. The Stoics noticed that you can have an impression—say, of shimmering water on a desert road—without judging that things really are as they seem. Judgement is the acceptance (or rejection) of an impression; knowledge is wise judgement, or the acceptance of just the right impressions. In the Stoic view, people make mistakes and fall short of knowledge when they accept poor impressions—say, when you judge that some friend is approaching, on the basis of a hazy glimpse of someone in the distance. When an impression is unclear, you might be wrong—or even if you are right, you are just lucky to be hitting the mark. A lucky guess does not amount to knowledge. The wise person would wait until that friend was closer and could be seen clearly. Indeed, according to the Stoics, you attain knowledge only when you accept an impression that is so clear and distinct that you couldn't be mistaken.

Academic Sceptics were happy to agree that knowledge would consist in accepting only impressions that couldn't be wrong, but they proceeded to argue that there simply are no such impressions. Would it be enough to wait until your friend comes nearer? Remember that people can have identical twins, with features so similar that you can't tell them apart, even close up. If you feel sure your friend has no twin, remind yourself that you might be misremembering, dreaming, drunk, or hallucinating. If the wise person waits to accept just impressions that couldn't possibly be wrong, he will be waiting forever: even the sharpest and most vivid impression might be mistaken. Because impressions are always fallible, the Academic Sceptics argued, knowledge is impossible.

One might wonder about the internal consistency of this position: how could the Academics be so certain of the impossibility of knowledge while at the same time doubting our ability to establish anything with certainty? Such concerns helped to motivate an even deeper form of scepticism. Imagine a way of thinking which consists of *pure* doubt, making no positive claims at all, not even the claim that knowledge could be proven to lie out of reach. Pyrrhonian Scepticism aimed to take this more radical approach. The movement was named in honour of Pyrrho of Elis (*c*.360–270 BCE), who is known to us not through his own written texts—he left no surviving works—but through the reports of other philosophers and historians. As a young man, Pyrrho joined Alexander the Great's expedition to India, where he is said to have enjoyed some exposure to Indian philosophy. On his return, Pyrrho started to attract followers, eventually becoming so popular that his home town honoured him with a statue and a proclamation that all philosophers could live there tax free. Pyrrho's influence now reaches us mainly through the writings of his admirer Sextus Empiricus (*c*.160–210 CE), who drew sceptical ideas from a range of ancient sources to form the branch of scepticism now known as Pyrrhonism.

A central worry of both schools of ancient scepticism concerns the 'criterion of truth' or the rule we should use to figure out what to accept, assuming that knowledge requires not just accepting things randomly. Different philosophers have proposed different rules for deciding which impressions are the best ones, and if knowledge demands thoughtful choice, our criterion of truth itself can't just be chosen randomly. But if we can't be arbitrary, we need some rule to select a criterion of truth. Do we use our favoured criterion to justify itself? That looks like circular reasoning. But if we look for a fresh rule to justify our criterion, then we will need some further principle to justify that fresh rule, and so on into an infinite regress.

Pyrrhonians were happy to draw attention to the difficulty of the problem of the criterion, without positively claiming that it would forever remain unsolved. But having appreciated the difficulty here, they adopted the plan of general suspension of judgement. They developed a general strategy for generating doubt on any topic at all: whenever you are tempted to make up your mind one way on an issue, consider the other way. Instead of settling the matter one way or another (which would be 'dogmatism'), just continue the search for further evidence, keeping the two sides of a question balanced against each other in your mind. Many techniques were available for keeping contrary ideas in balance. You could think about how different things would appear to other animals, or when seen from other perspectives, or in different cultures. Drawing on the work of earlier sceptics, Sextus Empiricus developed an extensive catalogue of ways to keep yourself from settling for any particular answer to any given question. He also developed lists of phrases that the sceptic could say to himself ('I determine nothing'; 'Perhaps it is, and perhaps it is not'). Sextus did not want these phrases to be seen as his own expressions of dogma: his scepticism was laid out as a practice or way of life, and not as a positive theory of reality. Keeping all questions open may sound like a recipe for anxiety, but curiously enough, Sextus reported the impression that his sceptical practice seemed to bring peace of mind. (Only an impression, of course— he couldn't be sure that he had achieved true peace of mind, or that it had come as a result of the scepticism, rather than by chance.)

One early criticism of scepticism was that it would be problematic for human survival: if sceptics suspend judgement even on the question of whether eating will satisfy their hunger, aren't they at risk of starvation? The Pyrrhonians suggested that behaviour can be guided by instinct, habit, and custom rather than judgement or knowledge: in resisting dogma, sceptics do not have to fight against their raw impulses or involuntary impressions. Sceptics can satisfy their hunger and thirst on autopilot while refraining from judgement about reality.

The sceptical path of resisting all judgement is not an easy one to follow, and throughout the Middle Ages the dominant figures of Western philosophy were firmly non-sceptical. Scepticism did flourish in the Indian tradition, however, most remarkably in the work of Śrīharśa, whose 11th century text *The Sweets of Refutation* promised to teach its readers some spectacular techniques of argument that could be used against any positive theory whatsoever. Śrīharśa promised his readers that they could attain 'the joy of universal conquest' in their arguments by using these sceptical methods, many of which focused on the difficulty of defining the terms we use. Like the Ancient Greeks, Śrīharśa made much of the deceptiveness of appearances, and the weakness of our powers to discover the true nature of things. Śrīharśa also seems to have shared Sextus's hope of enjoying peace of mind upon abandoning all positive attempts to attain knowledge.

Radical doubts about the possibility of knowledge emerged periodically over the following centuries, most strikingly during periods of intellectual upheaval. As new scientific work challenged the medieval world view in the 16th century, there was a resurgence of scepticism in Europe. The works of Sextus Empiricus were rediscovered, and his arguments were eagerly taken up by philosophers such as Michel de Montaigne (1533–92), whose personal motto ('What do I know?') expressed his enthusiasm for Pyrrhonian doubt. This sceptical spirit was contagious: early in the 17th century, René Descartes (1596–1650) reported that, far from being an extinct ancient view, scepticism was 'vigorously alive today'. Descartes's best-known work, *Meditations on First Philosophy*, presents truly novel sceptical arguments about the limits of reason, alongside familiar ancient arguments about dreaming and illusions. In his deepest sceptical moment, Descartes invites you to contemplate a scenario in which a powerful evil demon is dedicated to deceiving you at every turn, not only sending you illusory sensory impressions, but also leading you astray each time you attempt to make an abstract judgement such as a simple arithmetical calculation. This vivid scenario has lingered in the philosophical imagination, even though Descartes himself thought that there was a sure way to dispel it. Descartes was not himself a sceptic (despite his considerable talent for presenting sceptical arguments): he took himself to have an airtight proof that scepticism is mistaken. His optimism about having solved the problem of scepticism was not widely shared, however, and the major thinkers of the Early Modern period continued to struggle with the problem. Chapter 3 will examine Descartes and his rivals more closely, looking at their treatments of scepticism in the context of their positive theories of knowledge.

Old challenges, fresh replies

The old question of scepticism received some surprising new answers in the 20th century. A strangely simple approach was advanced by the English philosopher G. E. Moore in a public lecture in 1939. In answer to the question of how we could prove the reality of the external world, Moore simply held up his hands (saying, 'Here is one hand, and here is another'), explained that they were external objects, and drew the logical conclusion that external objects actually exist. Moore considered this to be a fully satisfactory proof: from the premise that he had hands, and the further premise that his hands were external objects (or, as he elaborated, 'things to be met with in space'), it clearly does follow that external things exist. The sceptic might, of course, complain that Moore did not really *know* that he had hands—but here Moore proposed shifting the burden of proof over to the sceptic. 'How absurd it would be to suggest that I did not really know it, but only believed it, and that perhaps it was not the case!' Moore insists that he knows that he has hands, but doesn't even try to prove that he is right about this. After shrugging off the sceptic's worries as absurd, Moore aims to explain why he won't produce a proof that he has hands, and why we should still accept him as having knowledge on this point.

Moore starts by remarking that when he claims to know (without proof) that he has hands, he is not claiming that a person can *never* prove he has hands. Moore was willing to grant that there are special situations in which someone might reasonably prove the existence of his hands: for example, if anyone suspects that you are an amputee with artificial limbs (and you are not), you could let him examine your hands more closely to dispel that particular doubt. If you were really keen to prove your point, you could even let him feel your pulse or scratch you with a sharp object. But however well that strategy might work to dispel particular doubts about artificial limbs, Moore does not think that there is an all-purpose strategy for proving that your hands exist, a general proof that would dispel all possible doubts. The range of possible doubts is truly enormous. To take just one example, a fully general proof against all doubts would have to show that you were not a sleeping amputee, dreaming in your hospital bed after an accident in which you lost your arms. Moore is pessimistic about anyone's chances of proving that this (admittedly far-fetched!) scenario isn't happening. However, just as Moore thinks you could know that you have hands without being able to prove as much, he also thinks that your inability to prove that you are not dreaming does not stop you from knowing that you are not dreaming. Moore once again retains confidence in his knowledge despite the limitations on what he is able to prove: 'I have, no doubt, conclusive reasons for asserting that I am not now dreaming; I have conclusive evidence that I am awake: but that is a very different thing from being able to prove it. I could not tell you what all my evidence is; and I should require to do this at least, in order to give you a proof.'

In claiming to have conclusive evidence that he is awake, Moore is resisting the hypothetical push of the sceptic's reasoning. Moore actually agrees with the sceptic that *if* you are dreaming, then you will not know just by looking that you have hands. But Moore reminds us that the sceptic's argument rests on that big 'if': as Moore sees it, the person who knows that he is not dreaming (whether or not he can prove this) should not be troubled by the sceptic's worries.

The strategy of declaring that one has knowledge without proof may set off some alarm bells (is Moore declaring victory after refusing to fight?). It may also seem odd that Moore is willing to construct what he thinks is a very good proof of the claim 'External objects exist,' while simply turning his back on the project of proving the somewhat similar claim 'These hands exist.' There's an important difference between those two assertions, however: the first is general and philosophical in character, and the second particular and ordinary. Explicit reasoning or proof has a clear role to play when we are supporting general philosophical claims: we can engage in extended reasoning about exactly what it means for something to be an 'external object', and indeed much of Moore's lecture is taken up with detailed discussion of this issue. By contrast, an ordinary claim like 'Here is a hand' is so basic that it is hard to find simpler and better-known claims we could use to support it. (There is a parallel with mathematics here, where some basic claims are taken as axioms, not themselves in need of proof.) If the sceptic attempts to undermine our certainty about such basic matters, Moore would urge us to distrust the sceptic's fancy philosophical reasoning well before we distrust our original common sense. We could reasonably be alarmed by someone claiming to know a controversial philosophical claim despite an inability to prove it; we should not feel such resistance to someone who claims to know a simple observable fact about his immediate environment.

Even philosophers who are receptive to Moore's suggestion that there is something wrong with the sceptic's reasoning may feel unsatisfied with Moore's plain and stubborn insistence on his common-sense knowledge. Some have tried to identify more precisely what mistake the sceptic is making, while also constructing a positive defence of our common-sense claims to knowledge. One major strategy was advanced by Bertrand Russell, a colleague of Moore's at Cambridge. Russell grants one point to the sceptic right away: it is *logically possible* that all of our impressions (or 'sense data', to use Russell's terminology) have their origin in something quite different from the real world we ordinarily take ourselves to inhabit. But in Russell's approach to scepticism, now known as the 'Inference to the Best Explanation' approach, we can grant that point about logical possibility and still hang on to fight the sceptic. Russell argues that there is a large gap between admitting that something is logically possible and concluding that we can't rationally rule it out: we have rational principles other than the rules of logic, narrowly conceived. In particular, Russell invokes the principle of simplicity: other things being equal, a simpler explanation is rationally preferred to a more complex one. It's logically possible that all the sense data you ordinarily credit to your pet cat (meowing sounds, the sight and feel of fur, and so on) do not come from the source you expect. Perhaps these impressions issue from a succession of different creatures, or from a series of inexplicably consistent dreams or some other strange source. But the simplest hypothesis, according to Russell, is the one that you would most naturally believe: there is a single real animal whose periodic interactions with you cause the relevant cat-like impressions in the stream of your private experience. Just as it is rational for scientists to explain patterns in their data by appeal to simple laws, it is rational to explain patterns in our everyday experience by appeal to a simple world of lasting objects (the 'real-world' hypothesis).

Russell's approach has its attractions, but a few worries may linger. Even if we grant that Inference to the Best Explanation is generally a rational strategy, we might feel that it seems insufficiently conclusive to ground *knowledge* as opposed to just rational belief. This potential weakness of Inference to the Best Explanation can be illuminated by thinking about other contexts in which this style of reasoning is used. For example, a detective might use Inference to the Best Explanation when investigating a crime: once he has found mud matching the crime scene on the butler's shoes, heard the maid's testimony about the butler's hatred of the victim, and discovered a bloody knife under the butler's bed, the detective could reasonably conclude that the best explanation of the available evidence is that the butler committed the murder. However, the sceptic could point out, things might not be as they seem: perhaps the maid has committed the murder and very skilfully framed the innocent butler. This is not the simplest explanation, but it just might be the true one. Assuming that the detective uncovered no evidence of the maid's involvement, it could be rational for him to conclude that the butler is guilty, but this wouldn't establish that the butler actually was guilty. Likewise, some sceptics might be willing to grant that it is very likely that our experiences arise from ordinary external objects, or even that it is reasonable to believe as much, without being willing to grant that these experiences give us knowledge: knowledge, they might argue, calls for a higher standard than rational belief.

A further worry about Russell's strategy is that it is not obvious that the real-world hypothesis really is a better explanation of our experience than rival explanations the sceptic might offer. A sceptic might argue that the evil demon hypothesis can neatly explain the very features of our experience that impressed Russell: *of course* an evil demon would send us vivid and apparently coherent experiences over time, given that the evil demon is trying to deceive us into believing that there is an outer world of objects. This objection applies equally well to other versions of the sceptical hypothesis. For those who resist the supernatural element of the evil demon story, there is a modernized scientific version available: just suppose that your brain has been removed from your body and connected to a supercomputer which simulates experiences of a coherent reality, sending signals along your sensory pathways. If the program is good enough, maintaining consistency over time and adjusting its displays to match your outgoing motor signals (you decide to look to the left, and your visual experience changes accordingly…), your experience as a brain in a vat might be internally indistinguishable from the experience of someone interacting with an ordinary physical environment. Everything you think you see and feel—the blue sky outside, the warmth of the sun—could be an element in the large-scale virtual reality simulated by the supercomputer. Assuming that the point of the whole simulation is to give you sensory experiences that perfectly mirror the sensory experiences you'd have in an ordinary physical world, the challenge to the advocate of the Inference to the Best Explanation approach would be to explain why exactly the real-world hypothesis is a better explanation of our experience than the brain-in-a-vat hypothesis. To answer this challenge, various suggestions have been advanced: for example, the American philosopher Jonathan Vogel has argued that the basic spatial structure of the real world is much simpler than the spatial structure of the brain in a vat's virtual-reality-within-a-real-world, making the real-world hypothesis a better way to explain our experience.

Even if Vogel is right that it would be somewhat more reasonable to take ourselves to inhabit the real world rather than a vat, we may still crave a more powerful response to the sceptic. Is there a way to show that the sceptic's arguments contain a deep confusion, or that the sceptic must be saying something that is not just implausible but flat-out *wrong*? In recent years, some philosophers have used tools from the philosophy of language in an attempt to attack scepticism more aggressively. The motivating thought behind this new approach (the 'semantic approach') is that we can find ammunition against the sceptic by looking closely at the way in which our words have meaning or link up to reality. In particular, these new arguments against scepticism have drawn on a movement in the philosophy of language known as Semantic Externalism, a movement that traces back to the work of Ruth Barcan Marcus, Saul Kripke, and Hilary Putnam in the 1960s and 1970s.

The key idea of Semantic Externalism is that words get their meanings not from the images or descriptions that individual speakers associate with those words in their minds (that would be 'Semantic Internalism'), but from causal chains connecting us to things in the world around us. For example, in Shakespeare's time, water was thought to be an element; modern scientists now characterize it as the compound H_2O. But even if the question 'What is water?' would be answered quite differently by Shakespeare, the modern scientist, and the average person on the street, we have all been interacting with the same substance. The Semantic Externalist contends that we can all refer to the same substance when we say 'water' exactly because our meaningful use of the word is anchored in our common causal contact with a particular substance. Because Shakespeare and the modern scientist have seen and tasted the same liquid, whatever they thought about its nature, we can now say that they mean the same thing when they use the word 'water'. Sometimes the relevant causal chains must run through other speakers: no person alive today has met the late French emperor Napoleon, but we can still talk about him, as long as we pick up our use of the word 'Napoleon' through sources with the right kind of causal links back to the man himself. Semantic Externalism is especially useful in explaining how speakers with different (and conflicting) ideas about something can still talk about the same thing: when Jill says that Napoleon was very short, and Bill says that Napoleon was actually above average in height (knowing that the rumours of his small stature were started by his English enemies), they can be discussing the same person despite the differences in their mental images.

The best-known application of Semantic Externalism to scepticism is found in Hilary Putnam's 1981 book *Reason, Truth and History*. Putnam's target was the sceptic who attempts to make you feel very worried that you might be a brain in a vat. Putnam argued that the sentence 'I am now a brain in a vat' couldn't actually be true for anyone who understands that sentence. According to Putnam, a creature that only ever had electronic stimulation of a virtual reality could not mean what we do by the word 'vat': because this creature has only interacted with simulated images of vats, his word 'vat' can't refer to something physical in the world beyond the simulation. Outside the simulation, our grasp of the word's meaning is anchored in our history of experiences with real-world vats. Our very capacity to make sense of the sceptic's hypothesis is a sign that we are in the real world: if you actually understand what vats are, it can't be the case that you have always been a brain in a vat.

Putnam's argument inspired an immediate backlash. Some said that it only deepened the sceptical problem: now we should worry that perhaps our words don't even have the meaning that we thought they did. Others noticed that even if Putnam could show that someone who had always been a brain in a vat couldn't talk about real vats, never having had the right kind of experience with them, Putnam's idea wouldn't work for a brand new brain in a vat. The sceptic isn't restricted to trying to make you worry that you *are now and have always been* a brain in a vat. The creative sceptic could try instead to make you worried that you have been a brain in a vat just since midnight last night: you could suppose that your life until last night was perfectly normal, and then while you were sleeping a mad scientist took your brain and hooked it up to his supercomputer, which simulates a virtual world very like the reality you inhabited before last night. Assuming it's a very good simulation, nothing in your present experience can rule this out, and, unfortunately for Putnam, Semantic Externalism delivers the verdict that your word 'vat' is still perfectly meaningful, with its meaning anchored in your past experiences of real-world vats. This 'recent vat' scenario still has the result that all of your present sensory experience could be illusory (you think the sky is blue, but it's actually a dark and stormy day, and so on…), and this is a disturbing result that the sceptic will be delighted to secure.

The 1999 science fiction movie *The Matrix* dramatized this problem for a large audience. The movie's hero ('Neo', played by

Keanu Reeves) discovers that his life as an office worker in the 1990s is just a simulation: it's actually two difficult centuries later, and human beings have lost a war against machines guided by artificial intelligence. These machines now keep humans trapped in pods, and, for reasons that it would be tedious to explain, feed them with synthesized experiences in a massive synchronized virtual reality ('the Matrix'). By discovering some weaknesses in the programming, and by getting some help from a few brave humans who have resisted the machines, Neo finds a way out of the simulation. He is offered a choice between continuing life as a comfortable office worker in the simulation, and breaking free of the Matrix to join the underground fight against the machines, a moment dramatized in the movie as a choice between taking a red pill (for dangerous reality outside the Matrix) or a blue pill (for continued comfort within it). Fortunately for the plot of the movie, Neo takes the red pill. But one might wonder what is at stake here. Why exactly would experiencing a world of physical objects be better than staying immersed in a computer-generated simulation?

Perhaps it wouldn't. This surprising answer has been vigorously defended by the philosopher David Chalmers, who argues that the brain in a vat (BIV) is better off than you might suppose. In particular, Chalmers aims to show that the BIV's everyday beliefs about its surroundings are *true*: when the BIV is stimulated by the supercomputer to 'see' a book, for example, and then thinks to itself 'I am holding this small book in my hands,' it isn't actually being deceived or making a mistake. The trick is just that the BIV's words and thoughts refer not to objects composed of physical particles but to something fundamentally computational in character. Picking up on the Semantic Externalist idea that links the meanings of our words to whatever caused our experiences, Chalmers proposes that when the BIV talks about 'this small book' or 'my hands', it is actually referring to the subroutines in the supercomputer that are responsible for its relevant sensations of white paper and grasping fingers. This means the BIV is *right* to say that it is holding the book, given the nature of its experiences—the part of the supercomputer's program responsible for the book experiences is indeed going to be linked up to the part responsible for his hand experiences in a way that constitutes 'holding' for the BIV, the only kind of holding the BIV has ever known. From our perspective outside the vat, we'd say that the BIV is virtually holding a virtual book, but from within, the BIV is right to say and think that it is holding a book: its words have meanings appropriate to its environment, and given those meanings, what the BIV believes is true. In fact, nothing stops the BIV from *knowing* that it is holding (what it would call) a book. The 'sceptical scenario' doesn't really threaten everyday knowledge at all.

On this way of thinking, a virtual reality that is ultimately computational in character is no worse than a physical reality that is ultimately composed of subatomic particles. It might surprise us to discover that we inhabit such a reality, but if Chalmers is right, such a discovery would be like the discovery that quantum mechanics or string theory is true: we might be momentarily unsettled to hear that the ultimate nature of things is stranger than we had previously imagined, but the news should not shake our faith in our ordinary knowledge about shoes, hands, and books. (You care whether your shoes are wet or uncomfortable, but do you really care whether your shoes are ultimately composed of point-like particles, vibrating one-dimensional objects, or instructions in a computer program? Chalmers thinks: probably not.)

The sceptic wants to use the BIV scenario to scare us into thinking that there is no knowledge: 'You can't possibly rule out a situation in which most of your beliefs are false.' Unlike Moore, Chalmers agrees with the sceptic that the BIV scenario can't be ruled out, but he fights back against the suggestion that most of our beliefs would be false in such a situation. However, we might worry about variations on the sceptical scenario: like Putnam, Chalmers has difficulty with cases involving subjects very newly immersed in a virtual reality. Because they have known in the past what it is to physically hold a non-virtual book, and because the meanings of their words are anchored to their past experiences, they will be saying something false when their newly attached supercomputer gives them virtual reality experiences of a virtual book: when the fledgling BIV says 'I am holding a book,' it will mean a real, particle-based book, and what it says will therefore be false, and it will fail to have knowledge. Chalmers is very much aware of this worry, but seeks to soften its impact by pointing out that the newly envatted BIV will still have extensive knowledge of its past. If Chalmers is right, the sceptic can't easily generate a sweeping all-purpose scenario in which *almost all* of your beliefs about your past, present, and future are false. The persistent sceptic could still point out that his main knowledge-undermining purposes can be served pretty nicely by a milder scenario in which you are just (for example) wrong about everything you now perceive. If you've just been hooked up to a supercomputer that is simulating your experiences, then even Chalmers will admit that you can't know whether you are now wearing shoes. Meanwhile, you might continue to worry that your inability to rule out this scenario should undermine your claim to know such a fact already, whether or not you are in a simulation.

Is it hopeless to try to argue against the sceptic in the first place? In contrast to the ambitious project of attacking the sceptic's reasoning, some philosophers have advocated a more defensive approach, according to which we must resist the temptation to try to answer the sceptic on his own terms, and instead aim to stay out of his reach in the first place. Given that the sceptic has promised to raise doubts about everything you say, there is not much hope for finding common ground with him on the basis of which you will convince him that he is mistaken. Those who choose to start with only premises the sceptic accepts will have trouble digging themselves out of the pit. Those who choose instead to start from a common-sense world view have the easier task of building some defence mechanisms against the charms of scepticism, while accepting our common-sense assumption that there is a good deal we know.

One way to defend yourself against scepticism is to come up with a diagnosis of why it seems so appealing, despite its tendency to lead us towards strange or even absurd conclusions. Various proposals have been advanced. Oxford philosopher Timothy Williamson suggests that scepticism initially looks appealing (despite its bleak consequences) because it is a good thing carried too far. The good thing is that we have a healthy critical ability to double-check individual things we believe by suspending judgement in them temporarily to see whether they really fit with the rest of what we know. But if this ability to suspend individual beliefs serves as a useful immune system to weed out inconsistent and ungrounded ideas, scepticism is like an autoimmune disease in which the protective mechanism goes too far and attacks the healthy parts of the organism. Once we have suspended too much—for example, once we have brought into doubt the reality of the whole outer world—we no longer have the resources to reconfirm or support any of the perfectly reasonable things we believe.

Other factors may also play a role in the appeal of scepticism. Perhaps there is something wrong with the basic model of knowledge that forms the background of so much sceptical argument. On this model, inherited from Stoicism, we start with impressions (or ideas, or sense data), and then we have a distinct stage of accepting or rejecting them. If we agree that the impressions received in real life and dreams or simulations seem just the same to us, it's not obvious how we could ever do a good job of choosing which ones to accept. This question loomed especially large in philosophy during the Early Modern period.

Chapter 3
Rationalism and empiricism

The Early Modern period

In many fields—literature, music, architecture—the label 'Modern' stretches back to the early 20th century. Philosophy is odd in starting its Modern period almost 400 years earlier. This oddity is explained in large measure by a radical 16th century shift in our understanding of nature, a shift that also transformed our understanding of knowledge itself. On our Modern side of this line, thinkers as far back as Galileo Galilei (1564–1642) are engaged in research projects recognizably similar to our own. If we look back to the Pre-Modern era, we see something alien: this era features very different ways of thinking about how nature worked, and how it could be known.

To sample the strange flavour of pre-Modern thinking, try the following passage from the Renaissance thinker Paracelsus (1493–1541):

> The whole world surrounds man as a circle surrounds one point. From this it follows that all things are related to this one point, no differently from an apple seed which is surrounded and preserved by the fruit... Everything that astronomical theory has profoundly fathomed by studying the planetary aspects and the stars... can also be applied to the firmament of the body.

Thinkers in this tradition took the universe to revolve around humanity, and sought to gain knowledge of nature by finding parallels between us and the heavens, seeing reality as a symbolic work of art composed with us in mind (see Figure 3).

By the 16th century, the idea that everything revolved around and reflected humanity was in danger, threatened by a number of unsettling discoveries, not least the proposal, advanced by Nicolaus Copernicus (1473–1543), that the earth was not actually at the centre of the universe. The old tradition struggled against the rise of the new. Faced with the news that Galileo's telescopes had detected moons orbiting Jupiter, the traditionally minded scholar Francesco Sizzi argued that such observations were obviously mistaken. According to Sizzi, there could not possibly be more than seven 'roving planets' (or heavenly bodies other than the stars), given that there are seven holes in an animal's head (two eyes, two ears, two nostrils and a mouth), seven metals, and seven days in a week.

Sizzi didn't win that battle. It's not just that we agree with Galileo that there are more than seven things moving around in the solar system. More fundamentally, we have a different way of thinking about nature and knowledge. We no longer expect there to be any special human significance to natural facts ('Why seven planets as opposed to eight or 15?') and we think knowledge will be gained by systematic and open-minded observations of nature rather than the sorts of analogies and patterns to which Sizzi appeals. However, the transition into the Modern era was not an easy one. The pattern-oriented ways of thinking characteristic of pre-Modern thought naturally appeal to meaning-hungry creatures like us. These ways of thinking are found in a great variety of cultures: in classical Chinese thought, for example, the five traditional elements (wood, water, fire, earth, and metal) are matched up with the five senses in a similar correspondence between the inner and the outer. As a further attraction, pre-Modern views often fit more smoothly with our everyday

31

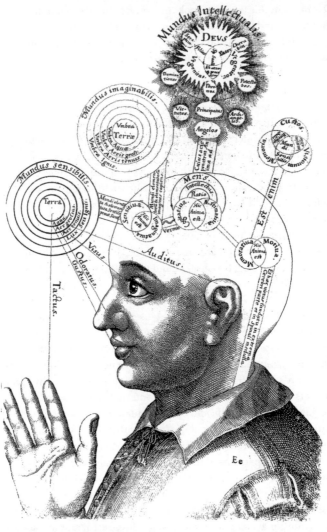

3. The Paracelsian view of our relationship to the universe

sense experience: naively, the earth looks to be stable and fixed while the sun moves across the sky, and it takes some serious discipline to convince oneself that the mathematically more simple models (like the sun-centred model of the solar system) are right.

For a brief period in the Renaissance the old and new ways of thinking fought for dominance. The conflict between these ways of thinking drove some philosophers to scepticism. Looking at the clash between the old theory that put the earth at the centre of everything and the new theory that the earth revolved around the sun, Montaigne decided that the only sensible path was not to take sides either way. But not all philosophers were happy to stay on the sidelines: some wanted to fight for the new, scientific way of thinking.

The Rationalism of René Descartes

Born in France in 1596, Descartes (see Figure 4) received a traditional Jesuit education, steeped in the classical ideas of Aristotle and his medieval interpreters. When he was later exposed to the newly emerging ways of studying nature, he had second thoughts about what he had learned in school. His *Meditations* begins with the confession that he had swallowed a 'large number of falsehoods' as a child. 'I realized,' he continues, 'that it was necessary, once in the course of my life, to demolish everything completely and start again right from the foundations if I wanted to establish anything at all in the sciences that was stable and likely to last.' The demolition programme that Descartes maps out in the *Meditations* was the method of systematic scepticism mentioned in Chapter 2, starting with small doubts about sensory illusions and finally rising to the all-consuming doubt generated by the evil demon scenario. By the time the evil demon appears at the end of the First Meditation, the narrator announces that he has succeeded in wiping the slate clean: he has generated doubts about all of his prior opinions.

4. René Descartes, 1596–1650

The remaining five Meditations carefully reconstruct a new world view on what Descartes hopes will be an unshakable basis. The first truth that can be known with utter certainty is the fact of one's own existence: whether or not an evil demon is tricking you at every step, you can never be mistaken about the fact that you yourself exist, and are a thinking being, at the moment when you think to yourself that you do exist. So far so good. But if 'I exist' seems like a slim basis to support the rest of what can be known, Descartes has an interesting trick for getting extra mileage out of it. In the Third Meditation he raises a reflective question: what was it, exactly, that enabled him to know that first fact? There was nothing more, he says, than 'a clear and distinct perception of what I was asserting'. If that is right, then we should be able to trust the rule *Whatever is clear and distinct is true*—for if this rule itself were fallible, we would not have a good basis to claim knowledge even of our own existence, Descartes reasons. The Third Meditation then bravely sets out to defend this general rule.

Without having established anything more than the fact of his own existence, Descartes has sharply limited resources to draw on, but as he continues to look within himself, he discovers that he has a variety of ideas in his mind, and he starts an inventory. Without yet deciding whether they represent anything real, Descartes notices that there are striking differences among his ideas. They differ in the kinds of things they represent (angels, men, the sun, the sky, God) and in their apparent origins. Some ideas (like his idea of the fireplace which is apparently warming him) seem to come from external things. Some ideas (like his idea of the hippogriff, a flying eagle-headed horse) seem to be invented, and others (like his idea of truth) seem to be built into him, or innate. As long as Descartes is worried that the evil demon might be deceiving him at every turn, it seems impossible for him to establish that any idea of his really does have the source it seems to have. But Descartes at last finds what seems like a way forward in the recognition that his different ideas represent greater and lesser things. Among all of his ideas, there is one that stands out to him at the top of the scale: his idea of God, an infinite and perfect being. The idea of perfection couldn't possibly come from any less-than-perfect source, Descartes reasons, and he concludes that this idea must come from God himself, and must be innate, planted within us from the start. Descartes's way of arguing from the mere idea of God to the real existence of God involves an appeal to a causal principle that not all of his readers have found wholly convincing (the principle that perfection, even in a mere idea, can never be caused by a less-than-perfect source). But once the existence of God is taken as established, Descartes moves swiftly to argue that all of our clear and distinct ideas (like our ideas of truth, numbers, and pure geometrical forms) are innate and entirely trustworthy. A perfect (and therefore benevolent) God would not have installed defective innate ideas in us.

If we have innate clear and distinct ideas that are perfectly trustworthy, it is an interesting question how we can ever make mistakes (as we obviously do). Descartes's next task is to tease apart the sources of error from the purely trustworthy core of our clear and distinct ideas. Some ideas, says Descartes, are obscure and confused rather than clear and distinct. There is some meaning in raw sensations like hunger, thirst, or even the sensations of colour and scent, but these ideas do not show us the true nature of things as they are in themselves. You can be wrong about the colour of an object in dim lighting, because colour ideas are not clear and distinct. By contrast, a clear and distinct idea like your idea of the number five, or the shape of a triangle, cannot fail to show you the nature of the thing it represents: you do not have to worry that your idea of the number five is misrepresenting that number. Echoing Stoic ways of thinking, Descartes contends that we are at risk of error when we make judgements on the basis of what is obscure and confused: as long as we stick to the clear and distinct we cannot fail. The best way to gain knowledge of something confused like scent or colour would be to analyse it in clear mathematical or geometrical terms (as we Moderns now do, explaining scents in terms of the shapes of molecules, and colours in terms of measurable wavelengths of light).

Known as rationalism, this way of thinking puts abstract concepts at the heart of our pursuit of knowledge. Descartes, whose own contributions to algebra and geometry were substantial (and included the development of Cartesian coordinates in geometry), was keen to defend the Modern enterprise of using mathematical tools to analyse nature. However, he still faced some difficulties in explaining the source of human error, an especially tricky project given his reliance on the claim that our innate intellectual hardware comes from a perfect God. In the Fourth Meditation, Descartes argues that God cannot be blamed for our mistakes, because these mistakes arise as a consequence of our freedom—in this case, human freedom to accept ideas that are less than clear and distinct. Freedom is, of course, not a bad thing, and any abuse of it is our fault, and not God's. It remains a mystery at this point, however, why God ever gives us obscure and confused bodily sensations alongside our brilliant and perfectly accurate mathematical and abstract ideas. It is only when he reaches the Sixth and final Meditation that Descartes at last tackles the difficult question of the point of our sensations.

Within the mind, Descartes suggests, we have various powers, including not only the intellect, which is responsible for abstract operations like those in arithmetic and deductive geometry, but also the imagination. To appreciate the difference in these powers, Descartes urges the reader to think of a chiliagon, a geometrical figure with exactly 1,000 sides. Intellectually, you can do this with perfect precision, appreciating the exact difference between a chiliagon and a 1,001-sided figure, or even calculating, if you remember the right formula, that a chiliagon has internal angles summing to exactly 1,996 right angles. But the imagination is rougher: when you try to visualize a chiliagon, Descartes predicts you will come up with something more confused, a figure with many, many sides, hard to tell apart from any other figure with many, many sides. Descartes concludes that the imagination is not simply reading the clear and distinct ideas in the intellect, but is oriented towards something else—the bodily senses.

The purpose of our sensations and related powers of imagination, Descartes ultimately concludes, is not to show our souls the true natures of things as they are in themselves (that job is reserved for the intellect); rather, sensations serve the interests of the body and soul taken together. Sensations like hunger, pain, scent, and colour help to ensure our bodily survival, which is itself something that a benevolent God could, of course, have wanted to protect. We can avoid being misled by our sensations if we keep in mind that they are not designed to show the true nature of things; rather, their deliverances need to be checked against and interpreted in the light of our clear and distinct ideas. We can separate dreams from waking life by observing the consistency and coherence of what we really experience, reassured by the thought that a benevolent God would not have left us trapped in a lifelong dream. Knowledge is possible when we coordinate our mental powers carefully, subjecting our confused sensations to the discipline of our innate rationality.

Descartes himself was extremely optimistic about his rationalist system, claiming in his preface that his proofs were 'of such a kind that I reckon they leave no room for the possibility that the human mind will ever discover better ones'. His enthusiasm was not universally shared. Few of his critics doubted his claims about the certainty of one's own existence, but there was considerable resistance to his arguments beyond that point. The theologian Antoine Arnauld immediately worried that Descartes was reasoning in a circle in the Third Meditation, needing to rely on clear and distinct ideas in the course of his proof that clear and distinct ideas were in fact trustworthy (this problem, known as the 'Cartesian Circle', continues to haunt Descartes's reputation among philosophers to this day). Princess Elizabeth of Bohemia pointed out that Descartes was disappointingly far from having a clear account of how the intellectual soul could interact with the physical body. The English philosopher Thomas Hobbes pressed Descartes on the question of how exactly 'innate ideas' were supposed to work. This last criticism was then advanced fiercely by the English philosopher John Locke (1632–1704).

The Empiricism of John Locke

Although Locke (see Figure 5) studied some traditional philosophy as part of his undergraduate arts degree at Oxford, it was only when he came across the new philosophy of Descartes, several years after graduation, that he became seriously interested in the subject. Amid a variety of other pursuits, including the study of medicine and a successful career as a civil servant, Locke worked on a theory of knowledge to rival Descartes's, spending 20 years developing his main work, the *Essay Concerning Human Understanding*. The central goal of the *Essay*, as Locke explains in his introduction to the work, is to 'search out the bounds between opinion and knowledge'. Locke was convinced that he could figure out the limits of what is humanly knowable by using what he called the 'historical, plain method' to study the natural operations of the human mind. Beyond the limits of what could be known, Locke argued, human beings could certainly have faith or opinion, but they should neither claim certainty, nor attack those who differ in matters of opinion or faith (the promotion of tolerance was a large part of Locke's agenda in figuring out the limits of knowledge).

The 'historical, plain method' led Locke to challenge the rationalist admiration of innate ideas. Looking at how human beings actually make judgements, is it really obvious that we have rational ideas installed in us from the start? Rationalists claimed that some principles are embraced by all of humanity and must be innate ('whatsoever is, is'; ''tis impossible for the same thing to be, and not to be'), but Locke's observations of humanity led him to disagree. 'Who perceives not, that a child certainly knows, that a stranger is not its mother; that its sucking-bottle is not the rod, long before he knows, that *'tis impossible for the same thing to be, and not to be*?' Against the suggestion that such principles might be innate, but not yet noticed, at least by children, Locke declared it to be 'near a contradiction, to say, that there are truths imprinted on the soul, which it perceives or understands not'.

5. John Locke, 1632–1704

What could 'imprinting on the soul' even mean, unless it meant making the soul aware of something? Advocates of innateness might try to say that innate truths won't be recognized until a child gains the mature use of reason, but Locke objects that requiring the use of reason to discover a truth makes it redundant to claim that this truth is also innate or built in. It would make as much sense as saying that the idea of the sun is innate within us but also requires the development of vision before it can be noticed by the mind.

Where the rationalists had argued that the mind comes pre-stocked with innate ideas, Locke maintained that our first ideas come from sensation: the mind is 'white paper' before sensation begins to mark it. Through repeated experiences, children gradually become able to recognize objects and people, as their raw 'ideas of sensation' cluster into patterns. As our mental powers develop, we also gain what Locke calls 'ideas of reflection' from witnessing the mind's own operations. These two sources, sensation of outer things and reflection on mental activities, are according to Locke the only sources from which human beings ever gain the simple ideas that form the building blocks of all human thought. This experience-centred approach to knowledge is known as empiricism.

Although empiricist accounts of knowledge insist that the raw materials of thought must come from experience, they leave room for more processed materials from elsewhere. Having received simple impressions from sensation and reflection, we can combine them into new arrangements, forming complex ideas of more elaborate and abstract things like justice, property, and government, or dreaming up imaginary creatures or new inventions. Once we have crafted these elaborate ideas ourselves out of simpler components, we can have clear knowledge of various truths about them. For example, Locke thought that the claim 'Where there is no property, there is no injustice' was 'a proposition as certain as any demonstration in Euclid'. If you can't immediately see why, this could be a sign that the ideas that come to mind when you read the words 'property' and 'injustice' are not quite the same as Locke's. Locke himself defines property as 'a right to any thing' and injustice as 'the invasion or violation of that right'. His 'no injustice without property' line falls out pretty easily if you start with these ways of defining the key terms.

Of course, Locke recognizes that we aren't in fact all defining our key terms the same way, and maintains that the most frustrating debates about moral and political matters arise from people associating different ideas with their words, and not really from any deeper difference in the ideas themselves. If we could gain greater clarity on precisely which ideas we mean by our words, for example by analysing them into simpler terms, then we could clear up these merely verbal disputes and achieve greater agreement and more extensive knowledge.

Knowledge has its limits, however, even when we take the greatest care to define our terms precisely. Locke defines knowledge itself as 'the perception of the connection and agreement, or disagreement and repugnancy, of any of our ideas'. There are various ways in which ideas can be seen to agree or disagree: Locke calls these the 'degrees' of knowledge.

The clearest degree of knowledge is *intuitive knowledge*, and this is what we have when we immediately grasp the agreement or disagreement of some ideas ('that a circle is not a triangle'). A slightly more difficult kind of knowledge is *demonstrative knowledge*, in which the mind sees an agreement or disagreement among its ideas but only with the help of some chain of connecting ideas: our knowledge that the internal angles of a triangle add up to two right angles, for example, is demonstrative knowledge, because it runs through a series of stages.

The last grade of knowledge is what Locke calls *sensitive knowledge*. Sensitive knowledge differs from the other kinds in being concerned not with general truths or relations among ideas, but with the existence of particular objects that we experience. According to Locke, you have sensitive knowledge of the existence of the things you are sensing: for example, the clothes that you are now wearing. You experience something very different, Locke observes, when you are really feeling something as opposed to merely remembering it or imagining it: it's impossible to miss the difference between looking at the sun during the day and just thinking about it at night. Because sensitive knowledge links our ideas to reality, it might seem to violate Locke's general definition of all knowledge as the perception of agreement or disagreement among ideas. But it is possible to see even sensitive knowledge as generated by noticing the agreement of ideas, as long as we remember that ideas include ideas of reflection, generated by our awareness of our mind's own operations. Whenever you have sensitive knowledge (for example, knowledge of the existence of the clothes you are now wearing) you experience your own mental operations of sensing the clothes, which are quite different from the mental operations you'd have if you were just remembering or imagining these clothes. You recognize that this feeling agrees with your idea of sensation, your idea of being in touch with things that really exist in front of you now, rather than your idea of an operation like memory or imagination.

Locke doesn't invest much energy into trying to come up with a clear answer to the sceptic who worries that you might feel you are experiencing something even when you aren't, perhaps in part because he seems to think it's humanly impossible to maintain scepticism sincerely. Locke thinks that we are 'invincibly conscious' of the reality of the things we sense, and can at most pretend to be sceptical about it. Locke also puts a heavy emphasis on the adequacy of our knowledge for our practical purposes: if what seems to be real is real enough to be a reliable source of pleasure and pain, then you can be as certain that it exists as you need to be. For Locke, knowledge is above all a tool for the pursuit of happiness.

Knowledge is not our only guide. Locke argued that many of our actions are governed not by knowledge but by something weaker, namely judgement. Judgement doesn't give us certainty, according to Locke, but it allows us to hold that a claim is probably true—and in many cases, the probability is high enough that we can treat it as practically certain. What we believe on the testimony of others, for example, is according to Locke always a matter of judgement rather than knowledge (a controversial claim, as we'll see in Chapter 6).

Locke's empiricism and Descartes's rationalism emphasize different aspects of the new way of thinking about nature that emerges in the Early Modern period. Descartes focuses on the importance of mathematical and abstract ideas; Locke focuses on the importance of experience and observation. Given that these thinkers both share the Early Modern agenda of supporting the new scientific way of thinking, how did they come to produce such different theories of knowledge? One possible reason is that they attack the problem of knowledge from different angles. In the *Meditations*, Descartes takes very much a first-person approach: his guiding question is: 'What can I know for certain?' Starting from his inner consciousness of his own existence, he then gradually moves outward by means of an inventory of the contents and powers of his own mind. From the first-person angle, the clearest instances of knowledge are those that do not depend on anything in the external environment: we can be confident of purely rational operations on abstract ideas even when we are unsure of the outer world. Locke shares some of Descartes's introspective tendencies, but he is also happy to adopt a third-person approach in many passages, drawing on his observations of others alongside himself. The main question Locke aims to answer is: 'What do human beings know?' How does the child come to recognize the difference between its sucking-bottle and the rod? From the third-person angle, we naturally take for granted the fact that the child is experiencing something real when we see him react to the sucking-bottle. The third-person point of view makes sensory perception, seen

44

as a relation between persons and their environment, a very natural foundation for knowledge.

The ideal, of course, would be to find a theory of knowledge that explains both the abstract and the observational (and how they fit together). Making progress towards that goal seems to require a deeper understanding of the relationship between the first- and third-person points of view on knowledge, a problem that remains a very active research topic in contemporary epistemology, and is the subject matter of Chapter 5. In modern terminology, the choice between taking a first-person or a third-person approach is the choice between 'internalism' and 'externalism'. The importance of this choice became very clear in the 1960s, as philosophers struggled to answer a surprising challenge to traditional ways of analysing the concept of knowledge.

Chapter 4
The analysis of knowledge

Gettier's challenge

Walking through the deserted train station on a Sunday afternoon, Smith realizes he has lost track of time. He glances up at the familiar station clock and sees the hands clearly pointing to 1:17, which is in fact the current time (Figure 6). If you are tempted to say Smith now knows that it is 1:17, wait a moment. Here's one additional fact about the situation: the clock is broken, and its hands haven't moved for the last two days. It's just a coincidence that Smith is looking at this broken clock at one of the rare moments when it isn't wrong. By looking at the broken clock, does Smith come to *know* that it is 1:17? Many people feel inclined to say *No, he doesn't know this*. (If you're not one of them, try the stories in Box 4 to see if they work better for you).

In a book published in 1948, Bertrand Russell offered the broken clock story as an example of a true belief which didn't count as knowledge. Russell included it alongside several other examples, such as a story of an man who buys a lottery ticket, feverishly convinced he will win, and actually does win. It didn't attract special attention at the time, but there is something special about the clock case. Fifteen years later, philosophers went back and took a second look at stories like the one about the clock, noticing a very interesting feature. Unlike the irrationally optimistic lottery

6. A stopped clock

ticket buyer, Smith is being completely reasonable: he has what
might seem like perfectly respectable evidence for his true belief
about the time. Ordinarily, if someone asks whether you know the
time, you just glance at your wristwatch and answer. You don't
say: 'I can't be sure whether I *know* what time it is until I
double-check that my watch is running properly.'

47

What prompted philosophers to think twice about the clock story was a very short paper published in 1963 by an American philosopher, Edmund Gettier. Gettier's aim was to challenge the way knowledge was analysed. The leading theories of knowledge in his day all equated knowledge with justified true belief (this equation was called 'the classical analysis of knowledge'). There were, of course, some debates over how the key terms should be understood; for example, over whether justification required a special kind of evidence, or an ability to defend a claim if challenged. But despite these controversies over the details, the fundamental structure of the classical analysis rested unchallenged. Gettier's 1963 article presented two stories which, like the clock story, illustrated the possibility of lacking knowledge even while making a judgement that is both true and justified (or reasonable, or supported by evidence). Philosophers had recognized for a long time that not every true belief counts as knowledge (even Plato talks about lucky guesses); what was new was the observation that even justified true beliefs could fall short.

If the man who looks at the broken clock has justified true belief without knowledge, the classical analysis is really missing something. It's not enough to add some justification to true belief if the justification and the truth of the belief aren't properly

---

Box 2 The classical analysis of knowledge

(where S stands for a subject or person, and *p* stands for a proposition)

S knows that *p* if and only if

(i) *p* is true;
(ii) S believes that *p*;
(iii) S is justified in believing that *p*.

related to each other: knowledge is something more than the simple sum of justification and true belief.

At first it seemed that the problem with the classical analysis would be easy to fix. One feature of the clock case you may have noticed is that Smith seems to have a false belief: he presumably thinks the clock is working, and he's wrong about that. Can we save the basic idea of the classical analysis by adding an extra condition ruling out reliance on false beliefs on the way to the truth? Perhaps achieving knowledge is like crossing a wooden bridge, where stepping on one rotten plank on the way across will make you fall short of the goal. A rule barring reliance on false belief would ensure that every step is sound.

This no-false-belief proposal was advanced within a few months of the publication of Gettier's article, and then immediately shot down from two different sides. On the one hand, people apparently *can* have knowledge despite the presence of a supporting false belief. Imagine a detective investigating a broad-daylight assault. She interviews a dozen witnesses who all say that they saw Jones hitting Smith, and then she gathers plenty of physical evidence, including blood droplets of Smith's type on Jones's knuckles, gets a statement from Smith, and even a confession from Jones himself. Does the detective now know that Jones hit Smith? Of course she does. (Only a sceptic would say otherwise.) But now try supposing that one of the dozen witnesses was lying in saying that he saw the assault (the others were all there and are being honest). If the detective believes that all the witnesses *including the liar* saw the assault, then she has a false belief supporting her judgement that Jones hit Smith. But it doesn't seem that this false belief is enough to bar the detective from knowing that the assault happened, given the extent of her otherwise solid evidence. The detective's one false belief is like a single rotten plank on a bridge that is so heavily reinforced with strong timber that it is still safe to cross. We don't (and shouldn't) follow a simple rule of denying knowledge every time a false belief enters the picture.

Further tricks can be applied to try to rescue the classical analysis. For example, we could try to say that our detective wasn't essentially relying on the testimony of that one witness: she would have thought the same thing even without him. Perhaps we can save the classical analysis by insisting that the knower can't *essentially rely* on any false belief (it can't be a crucial weight-bearing plank in the bridge). But it turns out to be very hard to explain what it means to 'essentially rely' on something in the course of forming a judgement—a blizzard of rival theories tried to work out that question, and none seemed to succeed. Meanwhile, there was fading enthusiasm for the whole barring-false-belief way of enhancing the classical analysis, because this approach was also failing on another frontier. Although Gettier's own stories happened to involve people with false beliefs, it turns out to be possible—as we'll see shortly—to construct Gettier-type stories in which a character has justified true belief without knowledge despite having no relevant false beliefs at all. While defenders of the classical analysis struggled to find a way to patch it up, others were inspired to propose entirely fresh accounts of the nature of knowledge.

The causal theory of knowledge

Walking into your neighbourhood bakery at the end of the day, craving a muffin, you are happy to see what looks like a full basket of muffins in the display case. 'Thank goodness they haven't sold out!' you think to yourself. What you don't know is that the basket you are looking at is strictly decorative: the 'muffins' you see are plastic fakes, attractively arranged to make the display case look good, and left there day and night, whether or not the store still has muffins available. As luck would have it, there are in fact a few muffins left in the bakery, out of view, on a shelf under the counter. Your belief that there are still muffins in the store is true, and—assuming that the plastic fakes are very realistic—justified. But do you know, on the basis of seeing the display case, that the bakery has not sold out of muffins for the day?

In this Gettier case there is some gap between the source of your justification (the plastic display) and the fact that makes your belief true (the muffins under the counter). A good theory of knowledge would do something to close that gap. In 1967, Alvin Goldman proposed a new and very simple theory promising to do just that. According to Goldman's *causal theory of knowledge*, experience-based knowledge requires the knower to be appropriately causally connected to a fact. What is wrong with your true judgement about the muffins, according to this theory, is that it is caused by your seeing the fakes. The fact that there are still muffins in the store is not what is causing you to believe that there are still muffins in the store. In ordinary cases of experience-based knowledge, on the other hand, the fact we believe has a clear causal connection to our believing it: when you have a clear view of the burning barn, that burning barn is causing you to have visual experiences that cause you to form your belief that the barn is burning. Memory and testimony can also connect us causally with facts, through causal chains linking us back to earlier events in our experience and the experience of others.

The classical analysis insisted that our beliefs have to be justified: this condition is conspicuously absent from the causal theory. Goldman's view is that there are many cases in which people should count as knowing things even if they can't now justify themselves by pointing to any supporting evidence. Average educated adults might know, for example, that Julius Caesar was

Box 3 The causal theory of knowledge

S knows that *p* if and only if the fact *p* is causally connected in an appropriate way with S's believing p.

('Appropriate' knowledge-producing causal processes include memory, perception, and inference.)

assassinated, even if they can't remember where they learned this fact, or give you any supporting reasons for their claim. The causal theory can credit them with knowledge as long as their belief that Caesar was assassinated has the right kind of causal grounding in the fact that Caesar was assassinated. An appropriate causal grounding could run from the fact of Caesar's being killed to the perceptual experiences of eyewitnesses to the event, and then through their testimony to ancient historians, carried forward through centuries of history books to the forgotten teachers who caused today's adults to have this belief about Caesar. It doesn't matter whether these adults remember exactly what their sources were; what matters is just that their beliefs actually have an appropriate causal chain anchoring them to the fact believed.

The causal theory was celebrated as a great advance in the theory of knowledge, but it harboured a few problems. Some critics worried about how exactly we could spell out the notion of an 'appropriate' causal chain without using the idea of knowledge itself, the very idea we were trying to define. Others worried that there was something wrong with divorcing knowledge from justification and evidence (more on those particular worries in Chapter 5). But one of the deepest worries came from Alvin Goldman himself, a decade after he published the causal theory. It turns out to be possible to tell a story in which someone *is* causally related to a fact in an appropriate way, but still lacks knowledge.

Here's the story: Henry is driving in the countryside with his young son, identifying landmarks for him as they drive past. 'Look, son—a cow! Over there—a tractor! There's a barn over there, in that field!' Henry's belief that there's a barn in the field is caused by his perceptual experience of the actual barn. By the standards of the causal theory, Henry knows that there is a barn in the field, and (so far) it seems that the causal theory fits common sense on this point, too: we'd ordinarily say Henry knows that there is a barn there, even if he doesn't get out of the car to walk up close to the structure and double-check. Barns are big enough, and distinctive enough, that you can generally tell that something is a barn from quite a distance away.

Once again, however, there's a twist in the case. He doesn't know this, but Henry is driving through Fake Barn County, where the zany locals have put up dozens of barn façades, false fronts that just look like barns when seen from the highway. It's sheer luck that Henry is right now looking at the one real barn in the region: if he had been looking at any of the other similar-looking things in the area he would have formed a false belief in taking it to be a barn. Does Henry know that what he sees is a barn? Goldman thinks not; Henry's risk of error is too high. Notice here that Henry isn't actually forming any false beliefs as he makes his judgement about that one real barn, and (assuming that he has no idea he's in Fake Barn County) he's also justified in believing that the roadside object is a barn. There's nothing wrong with the causal history of Henry's belief, either, so if he doesn't have knowledge, there's something wrong with the causal theory of knowledge.

Goldman at this point launched a fresh analysis of knowledge, focused not on causation but on reliability: the problem with Henry is that his ordinary barn-spotting mechanisms aren't reliable in Fake Barn County. On the new analysis, knowledge is true belief produced by a reliable belief-producing mechanism, where by 'reliable' we mean 'likely to produce a true belief'. Known as reliabilism, this analysis of knowledge rapidly won many fans.

Reliabilism also sparked criticism. One of the main criticisms concerns the key word 'likely'. If knowledge must be formed by a mechanism *likely* to produce true belief, what rate of success should count as likely enough? Would 85 per cent be enough? Or 99 per cent? The problem is not just that there are borderline cases where it would be hard to tell whether or not someone had knowledge. Lots of concepts have tough-to-call borderline cases, so it wouldn't be very worrisome if it were clear that 99 per cent reliability was enough for knowledge, and 97 per cent not enough, and we just had trouble figuring out what to say about 98 per cent. The problem is rather that some factors make it look like we have to raise the line very high, even while other factors drive us to lower it.

To see why a high threshold looks good, imagine that you have a ticket in a fair one-in-a-thousand lottery for a huge cash prize. The draw has just been held, but the winner has not yet been announced. As you wait for the announcement, do you know that your ticket has not won? Odds are 99.9 per cent that it has lost, but most people say that despite the slim odds of winning, they don't know that they have lost until the announcement is made. But if a 99.9 per cent chance isn't high enough for knowledge, how high do our chances need to be? (You can even push the number up from 99.9 per cent just by imagining a larger lottery—even with a million tickets sold, it still seems you don't *know* that your ticket has lost just on the basis of recognizing the long odds against it.) So, does your belief-forming mechanism have to be more than 99.9999 per cent reliable to gain knowledge by using it? If we insist on that, it looks like we are headed down a slippery slope towards scepticism: we want to allow that people can know things when they form true beliefs through ordinary sensory perception, even if it has a more than one-in-a-million chance of delivering a false belief. The reliabilist analysis of knowledge (true belief that is produced by a mechanism likely to produce true belief) is attractively simple, but it's not immediately obvious how to make it work (we'll explore the strengths and weaknesses of reliabilism in more detail in Chapter 5).

No way out?

Gettier showed that the classical analysis was missing something. Philosophers hoped at first that this missing ingredient would be easy to find, that we could just add a fourth condition to the classical three, or devise a new way of breaking knowledge down into simpler building blocks. These hopes have been dashed: in the decades after Gettier, dozens of analyses of knowledge have been formulated, but none has secured broad support. Many analyses turned out to be vulnerable to new intuitive counter-examples; others turned out to be disappointingly circular, essentially assuming the concept they were trying to analyse, sometimes under the disguise of newly introduced technical vocabulary. After three decades of increasingly complicated and unsatisfying proposals, some philosophers began to suspect that the problem of analysing knowledge was not solvable. But why not?

The answer may lie in the relationship between justification and truth. It's widely held that we can be justified in believing falsehoods: unlike knowledge, justification doesn't ensure truth. The person who is taken in by a very realistic holographic projection of a muffin isn't crazy to think that there's a muffin in front of her: she is being perfectly reasonable, even if what she believes is false or only coincidentally true. We could say the same for the investigator who ends up believing something false because he encounters tons of (misleading) evidence: given what he has found, he could be entirely reasonable to believe that the butler is guilty, for example. In fact, the possibility of justified false belief was part of what gave the classical analysis its original punch: if we ask which justified beliefs count as knowledge, the truth condition narrows it down to 'just the true ones'. But once we allow that justification doesn't always lead to the truth, the Gettier problem can start to look inescapable. There's now even a standard recipe for cooking up counter-examples to analyses of knowledge, courtesy of the American philosopher Linda Zagzebski. Here's how it works: describe a situation in which someone has a false but justified belief (or more generally, a false belief that fits all the conditions in the proposed analysis other than truth). Then add a lucky twist to the story so that the proposition believed ends up being true. Zagzebski's recipe has generated counter-examples to a massive range of proposed theories of knowledge.

Can knowing be analysed at all?

If efforts to analyse knowledge aren't going very well, it's useful to step back and ask why. Some philosophers have argued that the real problem here is that *knowledge* is not a well-behaved concept: Matt Weiner, for example, thinks that our use of the verb 'know' is guided by a set of handy but inconsistent principles. Trying to get a clear definition of knowledge out of the conflicting ways we intuitively speak of it is like trying to identify the make and model of a car composed of assorted scrap parts. Other philosophers have argued that we should shift our attention away from knowledge and refocus on other topics, like the question of what it is reasonable to believe. But it's not obvious that the difficulties we've experienced in analysing knowledge should lead us to turn away from it. Sometimes resistance to analysis is a good sign, a sign we have reached something fundamental.

To see the value of resistance to analysis, consider a case where resistance is low: table salt can easily be analysed as sodium chloride (NaCl). The building blocks here (Na^+ and Cl^-) are simpler than the compound they form together, and these basic building blocks can be combined with other materials to form different compounds. The project of analysing knowledge started with the idea that knowledge was also composed of simpler materials, including truth and belief. It's clearly right to say that truth and belief can be combined with other materials to make states that differ from knowledge—when beliefs are combined with factors like falsity, they fail to count as knowledge, and so on. But the other key assumption in the analysis-of-knowledge project is more controversial. Are the building blocks of belief and truth really simpler than knowledge itself, and is knowledge really a compound built out of those factors (perhaps with some other factors thrown in)?

Maybe not. In particular, it's not obvious that *believing* is simpler and more basic than *knowing*. What if *knowing* is the fundamental idea, and *believing* is a spin-off from it? This idea is championed by the 'knowledge-first' movement in epistemology. Leading this movement, Timothy Williamson argues that one reason why philosophers have not been able to come up with a satisfactory analysis of knowledge in terms of belief plus further factors is that the concept of knowledge is more fundamental or basic than the concept of belief.

There's something initially counter-intuitive about the knowledge-first approach. It can seem that believing just has to be a more basic building block for the simple reason that states of belief are more plentiful than states of knowledge. Every time someone knows something, they can also be described as believing it, but not vice versa: beliefs that are false or irrational, for example, aren't knowledge. To go back to our original analogy, basic building blocks are in many cases more common than the compounds they form: sodium, for example, is more common than table salt because sodium is present not only in sodium chloride but also in sodium nitrate and many other compounds (whenever you have table salt you have sodium, but not vice versa). However, it's not always true that the more common thing is more basic. Consider the concept of a perfect circle: very simple, and perhaps quite rarely found in nature. Now, if by the word 'rounded' we mean 'at least roughly circular', then there will be many more rounded things than circular things, but the concept of the circle would still be more basic. The circle is our fundamental starting point, something we used in defining 'rounded', and for good reason: the clean geometrical nature of circularity is simpler than the messy geometrical nature of approximations of circularity.

Box 4 Ancient Gettier cases

In Western philosophy, 1963 is taken as the date of the discovery of cases illustrating the gap between justified true belief and knowledge. But in a text that dates to around the year 770 CE, the Indian philosopher Dharmottara offers the following cases:

A fire has just been lit to roast some meat. The fire hasn't started sending up any smoke, but the smell of the meat has attracted a cloud of insects. From a distance, an observer sees the dark swarm above the horizon and mistakes it for smoke. 'There's a fire burning at that spot,' the distant observer says.

➢ Does the observer *know* that there is a fire burning in the distance?

A desert traveller is searching for water. He sees, in the valley ahead, a shimmering blue expanse. Unfortunately, it's a mirage. But fortunately, when he reaches the spot where there appeared to be water, there actually is water, hidden under a rock.

➢ Did the traveller *know*, as he stood on the hilltop hallucinating, that there was water ahead?

These cases involve a belief that is true and based on what could seem to be good evidence, and just like Gettier, Dharmottara uses these cases as counter-examples to rival theories of knowledge. Many cases like these were actively debated by Indo-Tibetan epistemologists following Dharmottara. Some of the proposals that emerged in Western philosophy since 1963 to handle these cases appeared in the Indo-Tibetan tradition centuries earlier. For example, a detailed causal theory of knowledge was advanced by Gaṅgeśa in the 14th century.

The relationship between knowing and believing is in many ways similar to the relationship between the circle and the at least roughly circular: knowing is the ideal, and believing is some kind of approximation to that ideal. According to the knowledge-first programme in epistemology, it is a bad idea to try to analyse knowledge in terms of belief plus further factors, just as it would be a bad idea to try to analyse the concept of a circle in terms of roundedness plus further factors. According to Williamson, rather than trying to explain knowledge as a compound state formed by adding various factors to belief, we should explain believing in terms of knowing: 'Believing p is, roughly, treating p as if one knew p.' In his view, knowing is a state of mind that essentially involves being right; believing is a state of mind that ideally aims at being right, while perhaps falling short of that target.

Because so much recent epistemology has been devoted to the task of analysing knowledge in terms of true belief plus further factors, it's somewhat revolutionary to declare knowledge to be more basic than belief. If analysing knowledge were the only thing that an epistemologist could do, then declaring knowledge to be basic (or resistant to analysis) would be a way of stopping epistemology in its tracks. However, even if knowledge is not a compound of belief and other factors, there are many things to be learned about it: for example, we can study how it relates to justification, how it is generated and transmitted through processes like perception and testimony, and how it appears when viewed from different perspectives. These issues continue to matter for both knowledge-first and belief-first approaches in epistemology. One of the questions that is agreed to be very important to both sides (and even to the debate between them) concerns the difference made by shifting from a first-person to a third-person perspective. The next chapter investigates the significance of this shift.

Chapter 5
Internalism and externalism

The first-person point of view

Here's something you probably took yourself to know before reading it here: Mount Everest is the tallest mountain in the world. But if that fact about Everest didn't come as news to you, here's something you probably don't know: how exactly you originally learned that fact (or any random trivia fact of that sort). According to psychologists who study memory, unless you had a pivotal life experience when you first heard that fact about Everest (like an earthquake hitting at the very moment it was mentioned in your first primary school geography lesson), you won't remember which source you learned it from. In fact, if someone challenged your claim to know that Mount Everest is the tallest mountain in the world, you might not be able to say much to defend it. You could say that it feels to you like a familiar fact. The challenger could object that those feelings of familiarity can be deceptive. For many people around the world, the claim that Sydney is the capital of Australia feels like a well-known fact. Sometimes, feeling sure you are right accompanies actually being wrong.

Suppose that a person isn't conscious of anything really justifying his claim that Mount Everest is the tallest mountain in the world. Could he still count as knowing that fact? Here philosophers split into two camps. The internalist camp says: If you really can't think of any supporting evidence, you are in trouble. Your belief about Everest can't count as knowledge if there is nothing accessible to you that supports it. It's unlike your belief that you are now reading a book, which you yourself can justify by appeal to the experiences that you are now conscious of having; it's also unlike your belief that there is no largest prime number, which you can justify by going through the steps of Euclid's proof for yourself (here's hoping you remember those steps). Knowledge is grounded by your own experience and by your own capacity to reason. Internalists place a special emphasis on what you can do with resources that are available from the first-person perspective: if you can't see for yourself why you should believe something, you don't actually know it. The subject's own awareness of good grounds is an essential part of what distinguishes knowing from lower states like guessing.

Meanwhile, according to the rival externalist camp, knowledge is a relationship between a person and a fact, and this relationship can be in place even when the person doesn't meet the internalist's demands for first-person access to supporting grounds. If it really is a fact that Mount Everest is the tallest mountain in the world, and if you really are related to that fact in the right way (more about 'the right way' shortly), then you know that Mount Everest is the tallest mountain in the world, even if you can't explain your reasons for thinking this. Externalists are happy to grant that *sometimes* you not only know something but also have special first-person insight into exactly how you know it. But from an externalist perspective, that insight into how you know is an optional bonus, and not something that must generally accompany every single instance of knowledge. Externalists argue that *always* demanding insight into how we know risks setting off a vicious regress. On the internalist way of thinking, they note, you shouldn't just have some random idea about how you know something, but should actually *know* how you know it (what is insight without knowledge?). But if knowledge always requires knowing how you know, then this second level of knowledge requires its own internalist guarantee (knowing how you know that you know), and so on. Suddenly you need infinite levels of insight to know the simplest fact. The internalist path threatens to lead us to scepticism, externalists suggest.

What part does the first-person perspective really play in knowledge? Is it indispensable to distinguishing knowledge from mere belief, or does insisting that it is indispensable lead to scepticism? Although there are signs of a struggle between internalist and externalist tendencies in epistemology as far back as the 18th century, direct debate about this question only emerged after Gettier's challenge to the classical analysis of knowledge as justified true belief. This challenge raised some serious worries about the power of justification, and prompted the development of prominent externalist accounts of knowledge like Goldman's early causal theory and his later theory, reliabilism, discussed in Chapter 4. To get a broader sense of how externalism works, it's worth examining one more influential externalist position—Robert Nozick's tracking theory of knowledge.

Nozick's tracking theory

Here's the fundamental idea behind Nozick's externalist theory of knowledge: the person who knows something not only has the right answer to a given question, but also *would* answer that particular question the right way, even if the answer were different. Imagine a doctor who tells you that you have contracted Hepatitis A. If this doctor just says this blindly to every patient she has, getting it wrong most of the time, then she won't count as knowing you have the disease (even if she's right, and you do). To count as knowing, your doctor should be giving a positive diagnosis to infected patients but not to the ones who are well. What Nozick's theory says is that there is nothing more to knowledge than this: if you have the tendency to believe something when it's true, and not to believe it when it's false,

Box 5 The tracking theory of knowledge

S knows that *p* if and only if:

(1) *p* is true;
(2) S believes that *p*;
(3) If *p* were not true, S would not believe that *p*;
(4) If *p* were true, S would believe that *p*.

then you know it. The theory imposes no special condition about awareness of one's reasons or grounds. The doctor who just has very reliable diagnostic instincts about Hepatitis A, even if she can't explain exactly what features of a patient she is responding to, will count as knowing whether you have the disease when she correctly diagnoses you. She can even count as knowing if she has a *mistaken* idea about how she's making up her mind. Suppose she thinks she's relying on the lab reports when really her judgements are based on subtle cues in the skin tone and smell of her patients: the tracking theory says that as long as her diagnoses actually track whether infected patients have the disease, then she still counts as knowing that they do.

The basic structure of the tracking theory is set out in four conditions: Conditions (1) and (2) are about what is actually happening. Conditions (3) and (4) are subjunctive conditionals covering what *would* happen even in circumstances somewhat different from the actual ones. According to condition (3), your belief that, say, you are now reading a book should be formed in a way that would be generally sensitive to situations in which you are not reading: it has to be the case that you *wouldn't believe you were reading* if in fact you weren't. The person who has constant delusions of reading doesn't know that he's reading even when he is. Meanwhile, according to condition (4), your belief that you are now reading has to be formed in a way that makes you generally alert to the positive activity of reading. It can't be some one-off fluke that you are right about what you are doing this time; you have to be generally a reliable witness about whether you are reading in order to know right now, in this case, that you are. Conditions (3) and (4) are the 'tracking' conditions on knowledge: in order for a true belief to count as knowledge it must be formed in a way that tracks the facts. Your knowledgeable beliefs vary in step with how things are in the world around you; not only do they match the world right now, they are formed in a way that matches how the world would be if things happened slightly differently. If you know, you are securely latched on to the truth.

The tracking theory has some tricky problems of its own. One problem concerns the methods we employ to gain knowledge. Nozick himself realized that there are situations in which the truth of a belief is awkwardly entangled with the method that we use to form that belief. His example runs as follows. Imagine Granny is in hospital, and her darling grandson comes to visit her. As he stands at her bedside, Granny looks at him and forms the true belief that he is well (or at least well enough to visit her). However, we can imagine that the family is so concerned about Granny that they would not let her find out if the grandson were not well (in that case, they'd tell her he was fine, so as not to worry her). So, if the proposition Granny believes (that her grandson is well) were actually false, Granny would be none the wiser: she'd go on believing he was well, violating condition (3) of the tracking theory of knowledge. Somehow it doesn't seem that this secret family plan about what to do if the grandson is ill should stop Granny from knowing that he is actually well enough to visit, as long as he is actually well and standing right there by her bedside. To deal with this problem, Nozick proposed an amendment of the tracking theory to include reference to a 'method of belief formation'. What the Granny case shows is not that there is any problem with Granny's method of belief formation (looking at her grandson at her bedside); the circumstances in which the grandson is ill are not circumstances in which her method would fail to deliver the truth, but circumstances in which she would no longer be in a position to use this method (she'd be using another method, trusting the testimony of her caring but deceptive family).

Like Goldman's reliabilism, Nozick's tracking theory ends up leaning heavily on the notion of a method of belief formation: you know when you hit the truth through a method of belief formation that measures up to certain standards. According to externalist theories, you don't have to know what those standards are; you don't even need to know what method of belief formation you are using. But it does have to be a fact that your method or mechanism of belief formation, whatever it is, actually tracks the facts (on Nozick's tracking theory) or is reliable in the sense of delivering a high proportion of true beliefs (on Goldman's reliabilism). But how is it decided what method a person is actually using in forming a belief? Externalism faces a difficulty here, acknowledged by Goldman as he first formulated reliabilism, and emphasized by internalist critics ever since. This difficulty has become known as 'the Generality Problem'.

The Generality Problem

Remember Henry, driving through Fake Barn County in Chapter 4? Goldman argued that although Henry's belief that what he sees is a barn is actually caused by the right thing (what he sees really is a barn), Henry doesn't know that what he sees is a barn. He's just lucky to be looking at the one real barn in a county full of fakes. Goldman's diagnosis was that Henry's barn-shaped-object-discrimination mechanism is not reliable in this context. In Fake Barn County, that mechanism delivers a false belief almost all of the time, so even though it's delivering a truth for Henry right now, he doesn't count as knowing: knowledge requires a reliable mechanism. It all works out neatly if we follow Goldman in saying that the context that counts is Fake Barn County (and not, say, the world as a whole), and that the mechanism that Henry is using is specifically his barn-discrimination mechanism. Reliabilism would not be able to deliver the desired intuitive verdict if we were to say instead that Henry is relying on a much more general mechanism, like 'vision', which could still be generally reliable, even in Fake Barn County. (Henry uses vision to tell that he is looking at the dotted line on the road, and the trees, and so on, and he's right about all of that—the County doesn't undermine the reliability of his vision as a whole.) We need to be more specific about the mechanism and context to get the result that Henry's belief formation is unreliable. But if we are being more specific, why not go all the way and identify the mechanism as 'barn-shaped-object discrimination, as applied to the barn-shaped object in the very spot Henry is now looking at'? Given that Henry is looking at a real barn, that maximally specific mechanism always gives Henry a true belief. But if we carve up belief-forming processes so narrowly, then any true belief will count as knowledge. How do we hit the target of describing the mechanism and its context at just the right level of detail?

Externalists have proposed many possible ways of answering the Generality Problem. One way already mentioned (if not endorsed) by Goldman in 1976 is to concede that there might be no simple objective fact of the matter about how to describe the mechanism Henry is relying on, because there is no objective fact of the matter about whether Henry knows. Looking at him the way Goldman does at first, Henry doesn't know, but if we take a broader view, perhaps he does. Theories which allow diverse verdicts are complex enough that we will address them separately, in Chapter 7. Another route externalists have pursued is to argue that there really is a natural way of drawing the lines around the process responsible for belief formation in any given instance. Many different proposals have been advanced, drawing on everything from patterns in natural language to the science of belief formation. Externalists consider this a vital and thriving area of research; internalists are sceptical that any satisfactory answers will be found.

Meanwhile, other externalists have argued that the Generality Problem is not exclusively a problem for externalists: internalists may also have to face it at some point. Internalist theories don't focus conspicuously on methods of belief formation: they talk much more about the evidence available to a person to justify or support what that person believes. But even internalists need to care about the manner in which a belief is actually formed, because all epistemologists care about the difference between having good reasons to believe something and actually believing it on the basis of those good reasons. Imagine a juror who has plenty of evidence that a given defendant is guilty of a crime, and believes that the defendant is guilty, but does so on the basis of racial prejudice rather than evidence. Epistemologists of all stripes would want to be able to criticize this juror's belief formation as ill-grounded. But as soon as we care about the processes actually responsible for producing your belief—and not just the evidence accessible to you—we will have to start developing some account of those processes, and we will have to find some way of describing them that is neither too precise nor too general. The Generality Problem seems to be everyone's problem, even if it is more conspicuously a problem for externalists.

Questionable methods

Internalists differ from externalists in assigning a special place to the subject's own point of view. To count as knowing, internalists say, the subject has to be able to see something for herself, simply by reflection or some form of immediate awareness. Different kinds of internalism differ on what it is that the subject has to see here, whether it is some justifying evidence, or completely justifying evidence, or whether the subject has to be able to know that she is justified. But the core idea is that the subject has to be thinking rationally, and making up her mind on the basis of evidence that is accessible to her. Externalists allow for the possibility of knowledge without evidence accessible to the subject, and they argue that this move enables them to defend the status of many beliefs we'd ordinarily want to classify as knowledge (like your belief about Everest being the tallest mountain). Internalists can go either way on that particular example. Some argue that it shouldn't count as knowledge (for most of us, anyway—perhaps experts in mountain geography truly know it). Internalists can say that we are speaking loosely when we describe ordinary adults as *knowing* that Everest is the tallest mountain, just as you might, speaking loosely, describe the shape of France as hexagonal—it's close enough for everyday purposes even if it's not literally a hexagon. Other internalists contend that we do in fact have internally accessible justifiers for beliefs of that sort: one can be aware that one's memory is good, that one has heard this claim many times, or read it in many sources, and so on. Even if some commonly remembered claims (for example about the capital of Australia) are wrong, internalists just need to say that the knowing subject has access to some justifying evidence; most internalists stop short of saying that the subject needs to have access to evidence of a kind that absolutely guarantees the truth of what is believed.

Internalism doesn't necessarily require the subject to be in the special insulated position of being able to know that he knows, or even to have access to evidence that guarantees the truth of what is known: milder forms of internalism can simply insist that the subject should have access to supporting evidence. Here's a story—from American epistemologist Laurence BonJour—to illustrate the desirability of requiring evidence for knowledge. Imagine someone ('Samantha') who thinks she has clairvoyant powers with respect to some odd topic. Samantha thinks that she has a supernatural ability to 'see' where the president of the United States is located at any given moment, although she has no good reason to think that she has this power. She hasn't ever checked up on the accuracy of her paranormal 'sightings', and doesn't have any good reason to believe that clairvoyance is really possible. One day she comes to believe that the president is in New York City, despite reading in her morning paper that he is at home in the White House that day, and despite turning on her television and seeing him give what is apparently a live press conference in Washington, DC. She dismisses all that ordinary evidence and goes with her sense of paranormal vision instead. Does Samantha know that the president is in New York?

Before you answer, here are some crucial twists in the story: the president really is in New York, and all the 'ordinary evidence' that the president is in DC is actually concocted to mislead the public in the face of a national security threat. Plus, despite having no good evidence about her special powers, Samantha is actually right: never mind how, she *does* have reliable supernatural access to the location of the president. On standard externalist theories, BonJour observes, Samantha is going to count as knowing: she is right and reliable. If her belief is formed by a reliable mechanism, it's not just a lucky guess. However, Samantha is being unreasonable in dismissing evidence that goes against her judgement, and in clinging to the deliverances of clairvoyance when she has no supporting evidence about its reliability. It's awkward, to say the least, when a theory of knowledge declares that someone who is being very irrational about some fact actually knows that fact.

Externalists have developed a number of different responses to BonJour's challenge. One possibility is to grant that it seems weird to declare Samantha to have knowledge, but then to insist that she really does know. The feeling of weirdness could be coming from the unfamiliarity of paranormal powers, or our learned cultural attitudes towards those who claim to have such powers. Externalists can also point out that any of us is really in Samantha's position when we start to form beliefs based on the deliverances of our ordinary senses: we don't have good reason to think that vision is reliable before we start to trust vision as a source of information. It remains disquieting that Samantha is ignoring contrary evidence, however. Another externalist response highlights that last point in order to challenge BonJour's claim of having developed a story in which someone is thinking reliably without gaining knowledge. If Samantha is deliberately ignoring counter-evidence to her judgement, then she's thinking in a way which doesn't generally lead to the truth (people who deliberately ignore evidence are generally unreliable). On this way of looking at the case, Samantha's belief formation does start out with one reliable component (the input of paranormal vision on the location of the president), but when we add in the unreliable way she is thinking when she ignores evidence, the total mechanism responsible for her belief formation is unreliable. If your overall method doesn't perform well by externalist standards, then the externalist has an explanation of why it seems you lack knowledge. Naturally, this way of answering BonJour's challenge leads us straight back into the thornbush of the Generality Problem (how do we figure out which way of describing the mechanism is the right one?).

A less confrontational response would be to admit that the internalist has a point here, and to soften externalism by adding an extra condition: instead of just requiring reliability or truth-tracking, one might also require that the subject not have any accessible counter-evidence of a kind that she would be irrational to ignore. Internalists have objected to this effort at compromise: why should we be so sensitive to the first-person availability of counter-evidence if we don't also insist on the first-person availability of positive supporting evidence? Another compromise position grants that accessible evidence is important for certain kinds of belief formation, while insisting that this is not because of a general first-person condition on knowledge. Contemporary psychology recognizes a split between two ways of thinking. We have a rapid, automatic way of thinking which delivers an answer without our being conscious of any sequence of steps (what is 7 times 11?—the answer just pops to mind). This is the kind of thinking that enables you to recognize the face of a friend or state a familiar fact. We also have a slower, controlled way which works through a sequence of stages (what is 7 divided by 11?—the answer takes work). This is the kind of thinking that enables you to solve a sudoku puzzle or figure out your income tax.

It's essential to the operation of this second way of thinking that you have first-person access to a series of steps. Many problems can be tackled either way: if you are asked what you ate for dinner yesterday, for example, you could just answer automatically and say the first thing that comes to mind (and you'll probably get it right), or you could reflect on it carefully and try to reconstruct the events around your meal and revive the detailed experience of eating it. We typically use the automatic way of thinking by default, but we can shift up to the more systematic way if we become self-conscious or anticipate needing to defend our responses (which is just the frame of mind encouraged by systematic reflection on knowledge, and the frame of mind we'd expect Samantha to be in when she struggles with contrary evidence). Internalists may be cheered by the observation that first-person accessible evidence is vital to systematic thinking, but externalists could also take comfort in the thought that automatic thinking is also widely taken to be a legitimate source of knowledge (for example, when you recognize a friend). Externalists can also argue that the reason why first-person accessible evidence is important to systematic thought is just that it is essential to the reliable operation of that mode of thinking.

As we move towards having a deeper understanding of what exactly is available to us from the first-person perspective, there is hope that we'll make progress towards figuring out the true importance of that perspective to the acquisition of knowledge. Meanwhile, progress can also be made by examining rival internalist and externalist theories of various special kinds of knowledge. One special kind of knowledge that is particularly useful to examine here is the kind of knowledge that is delivered through testimony.

Chapter 6
Testimony

They told you so

In the realm of knowledge, many of our prized possessions come to us second-hand. We rely on others for our grasp of everything from the geography of distant places to mundane facts about the lives of our friends. If we couldn't use others as sources, we would lose our grip on topics as diverse as ancient history (except what we could discover through our own personal archaeological expeditions) and celebrity weddings (unless we start getting invited). Testimony evidently expands our horizons: the challenge is in explaining exactly how (and how far). Does listening to other people—or reading what they have written—supply us with knowledge in a unique or distinctive way? Do we need special reasons to trust people in order to gain knowledge from them? What should we think about resources like Wikipedia, where most articles have multiple and anonymous authors?

At one extreme, some philosophers have argued that testimony *never* actually provides knowledge (John Locke will be our star example of this position). At the other end of the spectrum, some philosophers argue that testimony not only provides knowledge, but does so in a distinctive way. In this view, testimony is a special channel for receiving knowledge, a channel with the same basic status as sensory perception and reasoning (this type of position was embraced in classical Indian philosophy, and is now popular in Anglo-American theory as well). By exploring both extremes, as well as leading middle-ground views, we can identify the factors that are broadly agreed to matter most to how we absorb what people say.

No way to know

When does testimony supply knowledge? Some philosophers say: 'Never.' To see why philosophers might be sceptical about testimonial knowledge, even if they aren't sceptical about other kinds of knowledge, it first helps to clarify what we mean by 'testimony'. In an act of testimony, someone tells you something—through speech, gestures, or writing—and the content of what they are telling you plays a special role in what you get out of the exchange. Even sceptics about testimonial knowledge can agree that ordinary perceptual knowledge can be generated by the event of hearing or reading what someone says. For example, imagine either seeing that someone has written 'I have neat handwriting' on a slip of paper, or hearing someone saying 'I have a hoarse voice.' If you can indeed see that the writing is neat or hear that the voice is hoarse, you come to know the truth of what is said or written. But your knowledge here is perceptual, rather than testimonial, because the content of what is written or said plays no special role in what you learn: the sentence 'Smith got the job' would work just as well to convey the beauty of the handwriting or the roughness of the voice. If you believe something on the basis of my testimony, you understand what I am saying, and take my word for it.

For John Locke, there was a sharp contrast between perceptual knowledge (for example, the knowledge that a voice you are now hearing is hoarse) and whatever it is we get through testimony (for example, the news that Smith got the job). The key difference is certainty, which for Locke is a necessary condition for knowledge. Because perception can make you immediately certain of something, as certain as you are intuitively that red is not black, you can gain knowledge perceptually. What we get from testimony, Locke says, is at best highly probable, as opposed to certain. During an English winter, if you see a man walking across an icy lake, then you know that this man is crossing the lake. If someone else tells you that she has seen a man walking across the lake, then as long as your informant is trustworthy and what she says fits your own past observations, it is rational to consider the report to be very likely to be true, but you will not actually know that it is.

A key role is played by your own background experiences. Locke tells the story of the King of Siam hearing from a Dutch ambassador that water in Holland becomes solid enough in winter to support the weight of a man, or even an elephant (if you could coax an elephant to Holland in the winter). The king is said to have replied, 'Hitherto I have believed the strange things you have told me, because I look upon you as a sober fair man, but now I am sure you lie.' Locke is sympathetic to the doubting king: given all the king's past experiences in the tropics, it is entirely reasonable of him to find it more probable that the ambassador is lying than that water ever naturally becomes solid.

Even if testimony is never quite certain, it can still be more or less likely to be true, and Locke counsels maintaining a level of confidence in testimony that reflects the strength of your evidence. He has a complex formula for determining the perfectly rational degree of confidence in testimony: after first weighing how well it fits with your own experience, you must take into account the following six factors:

1. The number of witnesses
2. Their integrity
3. Their skill
4. The purpose they have in supplying their report
5. The internal consistency of what is conveyed, and the circumstances of your hearing it
6. Whether there is any contrary testimony

While he thinks testimony doesn't transmit knowledge, Locke doesn't think we should generally resist what others tell us: he says that the reasonable person will assent to testimony. When it fits with our own observations and scores highly on his six-point checklist, what we get from testimony is for practical purposes very like knowledge ('we receive it as easily, and build as firmly upon it, as if it were certain knowledge'). But what we get from testimony is unlike the discovery that red is not black, according to Locke, because it is open to being undermined later by further experiences. (You thought you had no reason to distrust her, but the woman who told you she saw a man crossing the lake was making it up, and later you hear from ten other people that the ice was too thin to cross today.) Locke argues that this vulnerability to future contrary reports means that what we get from testimony doesn't literally count as knowledge.

We'll look at a challenge to Locke's reasoning shortly. But first it's worth taking a moment to appreciate how radical his position really is. If Locke is right, then the proper answer to the question 'Do you know where you were born?' is 'no' (assuming that your beliefs on this matter are, like most people's, determined by what your family has told you, or what is written on your birth certificate). You could say that it is very probable you were born in a certain place, but not having retained first-hand experience of the location, you won't have knowledge of this fact. You also don't know that George Washington was once the president of the United States, or that Antarctica exists (assuming you haven't been there yourself). Lockean readers of this book can't even describe themselves as knowing that John Locke ever lived: they should at most consider it highly probable that he did.

It's clear that Locke is going against the way we ordinarily speak: we very freely describe people as gaining knowledge through testimony. ('Does Jones know that Smith got the job?'—'Yes, he does—I just told him.') However, we can recognize that in many situations the way we ordinarily speak is not strictly accurate (for example, when we talk of the sun rising or setting when really it is the earth that is rotating). Does Locke have good reasons of principle for saying that strictly speaking we do not gain knowledge from testimony? His argument about vulnerability to later doubts is questionable, in part because it seems to apply equally well to judgements grounded in perception and memory, which he does want to classify as knowledge. Locke thinks that perception enables you to know, for example, that you are now reading a book, and also to remember later that you were reading a book, retaining your perceptual knowledge through memory. However, it's possible here too that later on you will come to doubt yourself. Even if you are really perceiving something now, you might have doubts later on, perhaps wondering whether you were only dreaming. Locke doesn't seem to think that the possibility of stirring up later doubts should undermine your claim to know right now, as long as you are actually now perceiving and not dreaming. But a parallel argument could be applied to testimony: if someone knowledgeable tells you that Smith got the job, and you don't actually have any doubts about what they are saying right now, then you should now have the certainty needed for knowledge. If you start doubting later on, for example because of contrary testimony, you could lose that knowledge, but this is not proof that you never had it. If your informant was knowledgeable, then your later doubts couldn't show that what you originally judged was untrue: if your informant knew that Smith got the job, then it must be true that Smith got the job. Any report to the contrary is misleading. Of course, there could be situations in which you fail to have doubts, and take the word of a liar as if she were telling the truth, but these situations are parallel to situations in which you are taken in by a perceptual illusion. If there is a big difference between the knowledge-providing powers of perception and testimony, Locke hasn't shown us what it is.

The middle ground: reductionism

In claiming that testimony never supplies knowledge, Locke occupies a minority position. Most philosophers are more positive about it. The main moderately positive position is reductionism: we do gain knowledge through testimony, but the knowledge-providing power of testimony is nothing special. Whether we are reading, listening, or watching someone's gestures or sign language, we receive testimony through ordinary sense perception. Assuming everything goes well, sensory perception lets us know that a speaker has said a sentence. In order to gain knowledge of what the sentence itself says, and not just the fact that the speaker said it, we rely on our ordinary powers of inference and perception. There is still something Lockean about this: you look at the sort of factors on Locke's checklist for the likelihood of testimony being true (how well it fits with past experience, evidence about the integrity of the speaker, and so on), but when what you are hearing scores high enough, you come to know the communicated proposition. This way of thinking about testimony is known as 'reductionism', because the knowledge-providing power of testimony can be reduced to the knowledge-providing power of other sources, notably perception, memory, and inference.

Reductionism comes in two flavours: global and local. According to global reductionism, your own experience of the world gradually teaches you that testimony, in general, is a fine source of knowledge. As a youth, you ask for directions to the train station, someone tells you, and then even if you don't yet know the truth of what they said, you can follow the directions and confirm their truth for yourself. Because you can often double-check the truth of what people say, over time you gain knowledge of the track record of past testimony, which then works as a positive experience-based reason to accept present testimony. An ordinary adult can know that the train station is down the road and to the right as soon as he is told, not because testimony has any distinctive knowledge-generating power, but because his own past perceptions, memories, and inferences support accepting what he now hears. The global reductionist doesn't have to say that you should believe absolutely everything you hear: if you are in a situation where there are special undermining factors—for example, if you know that the person you are talking to has a strong incentive to lie—then you can take that into account. But when there are no special warning signs, the global reductionist says you have a standing positive reason to believe what you are told.

The local reductionist tries something more finely tailored: rather than seeking a blanket positive reason to trust all testimony, the local reductionist suggests that you look for specific positive reasons, in any given situation, to accept the word of the person you are hearing on the topic she is speaking about. Is this person an expert? Has she told you the truth in the past? How plausible is her story now? Again the specific reasons we rely on ultimately come from perception, inference, and memory, rather than on testimony itself. If these ordinary reasons are strong enough in a given situation, you can know the truth of what you are being told.

Both forms of reductionism allow us to say that most adults know where they were born and know that Antarctica exists. When testimony comes from close and trusted witnesses (like your parents, telling you about your birthplace) or from appropriate experts (numerous map-makers and travel writers, telling you about a distant continent), then it can supply knowledge, according to both forms of reductionism. In cases where you don't have any special reasons to trust your informant—lost in a strange city, you ask a total stranger for directions—the global reductionist can say that you gain knowledge, but the typical local reductionist cannot. (If you are lucky, the local reductionist says, you gain a true belief.)

Local reductionism can sound very calculating: in practice, we don't often weigh the reasons to trust someone before accepting their word. However, local reductionism about testimonial knowledge is not a descriptive theory about how we actually form our beliefs in daily practice: it's a theory about the conditions under which those beliefs deserve to count as knowledge. Even if we tend to trust strangers blindly when we ask them for directions, the local reductionist suggests that we shouldn't think of ourselves as gaining knowledge on this basis. Attaining knowledge requires greater caution, if local reductionism is right. Taking this line requires explaining just why we need greater caution for testimonially grounded knowledge than for knowledge grounded in perception and reason. It's true that testimony can let us down (sometimes our informants are dishonest or confused) but perception can also let us down (sometimes our eyes play tricks on us). One possible reason why testimony could be special is that it involves free agents who have purposes of their own. Human communication differs from the communication among bees, for example, who reliably signal to each other the location of nectar-bearing plants. A bee who learns the location of nectar from another bee is able to fly there as well as if it had witnessed that place: bee signalling gives bees the benefit of each other's experience, in what is sometimes called 'cognition by proxy'. Bee signals can be defective (if the bee is sick, or if the nectar-bearing plants are moved by an interfering researcher after the first bee's contact), but these defects are like the defects in our perceptual organs (when we are sick, or when things are moved behind our backs). One reason that bees can gain the benefit of other bees' experiences directly is that they cannot deliberately deceive. A local reductionist could stress that caution becomes important for communications between members of a sneakier species like ours.

Alternatively, local reductionists could dispute the suggestion that we often rely blindly on the advice of strangers. Perhaps we do ordinarily exercise caution, but in ways that are subtler than explicit weighing of the reasons to trust someone. Recent empirical work on 'epistemic vigilance' has advanced our understanding of how and when we actually accept the word of others. Even if we aren't explicitly thinking to ourselves about the reliability of the stranger we've asked for directions, we could be monitoring his facial expressions and speech patterns to assess how trustworthy he is. Better insight into our actual practices can help us see whether the local reductionist is in fact proposing an account that fits those practices quite closely, or instead proposing that our actual practices are sloppy and we don't have knowledge as often as we think.

Testimony as a distinctive source of knowledge

A still more generous approach to testimony is possible. Instead of seeing testimony as dependent on other ways of knowing, such as past experience and reasoning, you might think of it as a basic source of knowledge in its own right. According to the direct view of testimony (sometimes also called the 'default' view), when your knowledgeable co-worker tells you that Smith got the job, you know that Smith got the job, and your knowledge isn't dependent on your reasoning about the track record of testimony or the reliability of that particular co-worker. You just have to understand what a knowledgeable informant is saying in order to gain knowledge. It's true that the testimonial channel takes input from sensory perception (you have to be able to hear what someone is saying, or read what they have written); reasoning also takes input from sensory perception (for example, you look at a half-solved sudoku puzzle and start to work out the answer). But testimony remains a distinct way of knowing something, just as reasoning is distinct from pure sensory perception. The way you think when you understand what someone says is different from the way you think when you see something with your own eyes, and different again from the way you think when you are engaged in reasoning or puzzle solving.

The direct view of testimony dates back a long way: it is defended by the Indian philosopher Akṣapāda Gautama in the 2nd century CE. Gautama maintains that testimony is a special channel through which we gain knowledge, and emphasizes that testimony is not a form of inference. We do not think to ourselves: 'Lee has said that Smith got the job, and Lee is a reliable person, therefore Smith got the job.' We know, as soon as we understand what Lee has said, that Smith got the job (we can also focus on the fact that Lee was the person who told us about this, but that isn't the main thing we pick up). Unlike local reductionism, the direct view has no problem at all with gaining knowledge from strangers: the classical Indian line is that knowledge can be gained directly not only from sages and 'noble compatriots' but also from 'barbarians', as long as they have knowledge and intend to share it.

Contemporary advocates of the direct view emphasize that trust in testimony plays a large role in the acquisition of language and in our everyday practices of communication. Where reductionists and Lockeans think it is right to maintain a neutral stance towards public testimony until we can verify it with our private resources (our own perceptions and inferences), advocates of the direct view suggest that we do not have sufficient private resources available to manage that kind of verification. Vital knowledge of what words mean, for example, is made possible only if we can gain knowledge directly by being told something by another. We wouldn't be able to understand each other in the first place if we didn't start by trusting others to tell the truth and accepting what they say at face value. On this view, we drink in what others say, in something like the way bees do.

Even for the maximally generous direct view of testimony, there are still certain conditions that must be met: in order to gain knowledge, what your informant says must actually be true, and (at least according to most non-reductionists) your informant must also know that it is true, as opposed to just managing a lucky guess. Plato gives an example to illustrate this last point: he describes a slick lawyer who has to defend a client against an assault charge. This client is in fact innocent, but has no witnesses to back him up. Although the lawyer himself has no idea whether what he is saying is true, he does a great job of telling the jury that his client is innocent, using his charisma to make the jury believe him. Plato then raises the question of whether the members of the jury actually *know* that the defendant is innocent, on the strength of what they have been told by the charming lawyer. The answer to this question seems to be 'no'. If you are going to gain knowledge of a fact from an informant, the informant had better know that fact himself.

One of the leading contemporary theorists of testimony, Jennifer Lackey, uses the image of a 'bucket brigade' to illustrate this 'take it from someone who knows' condition on testimonial knowledge: '[I]n order to give you a full bucket of water, I must have a full bucket of water to pass to you. Moreover, if I give you a full bucket of water, then—spills aside—the bucket of water you now possess as a result of our exchange will also be full.' The 'spills' here could include cases in which you don't quite hear what I say, or cases in which someone has maliciously told you that I am a pathological liar, and you doubt me for that reason. Both in the classical and in the contemporary versions of the direct view, gaining knowledge by testimony can be blocked if you have doubts about the truth of what is being said, even if the speaker does have knowledge, and even if your own doubts are unreasonable.

Lackey herself raises doubts about the idea that testimonial knowledge arises only when we take it from someone who knows. Imagine a schoolteacher who has personal doubts about a true scientific theory that she is required to teach to her class (say, a 'young earth' creationist who is teaching the theory of natural selection, according to which humans have an ancient evolutionary heritage, sharing common ancestors with other primates). This teacher doesn't know that the theory of natural selection is true—she doesn't even believe it—but nevertheless she diligently teaches it to her class because it is part of the state curriculum. If the teacher's trusting students come to believe the theory on the strength of their teacher's testimony, couldn't we say that these students now know the theory? If Lackey is right, this is a case in which someone with less than a full bucket manages to pass on more knowledge than she herself possesses.

There are other ways in which less-than-perfect sources might be able to pass on more than they individually know. One way is by working with others. Right now, I'm inclined to describe myself as knowing that the Willamette River flows northward between the Oregon Coast Range and the Cascade Range in the American northwest. I know this because I just looked it up in Wikipedia (go ahead, double-check). It's possible that someone who actually knows this fact was the one who first updated the page about this river to report it. Perhaps someone with a full bucket has poured their knowledge through the Internet to me. It's also possible that the person who first reported the watershed boundaries had something less than a full bucket, and was, say, slightly unsure of the name of the mountain range on one side. However, over time, the entry as a whole has been vetted by so many people that the line about those mountain ranges is by now well-secured by the whole community of editors. This group may have succeeded in filling the bucket together, jointly generating an entry that is now able to provide the reader with knowledge. If the reliability of an informant is what counts, groups working together under the right conditions can outperform single authors.

This example would be handled differently by advocates of the different theories we have covered so far. A Lockean would say that what we really take away from reading the Wikipedia entry on the Willamette River is just highly probable opinion, rather than knowledge, even if there are many, many informants who are telling us something entirely plausible. A reductionist would say that any knowledge we gain here is really inferential in character: on this view, the article could transmit knowledge to those who are already aware that Wikipedia entries are generally reliable. For example, the entry could succeed in transmitting knowledge about the river's course to those who have read the 2005 *Nature* article

7. The suffering of past generations

reporting that entries in Wikipedia are comparable in accuracy to entries in the *Encyclopaedia Britannica,* or to people who have significant personal experience of double-checking the accuracy of Wikipedia entries. Meanwhile, a direct theorist of testimony could say that Wikipedia provides knowledge of the facts it reports (when its internal systems of quality control are working well), even to those who are unaware of the reliability of those systems of control. On this view, even a naive 12-year-old preparing a school report could come to know the names of the ranges flanking the river, just by reading the Willamette River entry. Traditional versions of the direct theory would require whoever wrote or edited the key sentence in the entry to know the facts it reports; however, the direct theory could also be stretched or modified to allow cases in which we gain knowledge not from a single knower but from a largely anonymous community including individuals with partial confidence rather than full knowledge. As debate about the epistemic structure of testimony continues, new channels of information afford fresh opportunities for rival theories to offer competing explanations of the social transmission of knowledge.

Theories of knowledge generally turn to testimony only after they have examined perception and reason, but there are some philosophers who place it at the very heart of their approach to knowledge. Most notably, British philosopher Edward Craig argues that humanity came up with the concept of knowledge for the express purpose of managing the problem of testimony: we use this concept to mark people as good sources of information. Craig starts with the idea that all creatures struggling to survive need true beliefs about their environment. It helps us greatly if we are not restricted to what we have experienced personally but can also learn from others. It's imperative that we have a way of sorting out good informants, who can serve as our eyes and ears, from bad informants, who are likely to lead us astray. Good informants are identified as knowers.

Craig reverses the usual direction of explanation: most epistemologists think that being a knower is something that makes you (potentially) a good informant. Craig, however, considers the notion of 'good informant' to be more fundamental, and vital to explaining both the value and the evolutionary origin of the concept of knowledge. Critics of Craig emphasize that knowers can sometimes be bad informants—knowers can be secretive or deceptive. In addition, there are some intuitions about knowledge that Craig's theory has difficulty explaining. For example, it is hard for Craig to say why we see the victim of a Gettier case as failing to know. The victim of the Gettier case will in some sense be a good informant—as someone with a justified true belief, he is getting it right and in some sense thinking reliably. Meanwhile, the evolutionary dimension of Craig's theory is also open to question. Research on our closest animal relatives has shown that they can distinguish knowledge from ignorance, but not in the ways Craig's theory takes to be most basic. In experimental settings, chimpanzees can't distinguish between knowledgeable and ignorant informants who give them clues about where food is hidden. Chimpanzees can, however, keep track of who knows what when they are competing for resources: for example, subordinate chimpanzees are good at remembering whether a dominant animal knows where food is hidden. The connection between knowing and acting seems to be easier to spot than the connection between knowing and being a good informant. While testimony is an important topic in epistemology, it's doubtful that it will work as our starting point.

Chapter 7
Shifting standards?

Counting on context

Some words are slippery. Every night, the word 'tomorrow' slides forward to pick out a different day of the week. 'Here' designates a different place depending on where you are standing. 'I' stands for someone different depending on who is speaking; and 'this' could be anything at all. Words like 'big' and 'small' are also tricky: a morbidly obese mouse is in some sense big, but in another sense still small. What about the verb 'to know'? Is it possible that it also shifts around in some interesting way?

What the other words featured in the last paragraph have in common is context-sensitivity. The context in which these words are used plays a role in setting what they stand for. Some words (like 'I' and 'now') are sensitive to the speaker's identity and location in time and space. Others (like 'big' and 'tall') are sensitive to a comparison class: it takes much more height to be tall for a skyscraper than it does to be tall for a cereal box. To complicate matters, the same thing could be a member of two different classes (mouse, animal): a creature could be big for a mouse and still small for an animal, and which adjective we should use for it depends on which of these classes we have in mind.

It's tempting to say that context-sensitive words keep changing their meaning, but that's not exactly right. We don't have to buy a new dictionary every day to keep up on what the word 'tomorrow' means. There are some fixed rules: 'I' always picks out the person speaking and the relevant sense of 'tall' always means 'large for its kind in the vertical dimension'. Rather than changing their meanings, context-sensitive words work like recipes that take input from a conversational context to settle what they stand for. Once the context is established, it should be clear exactly what 'this' indicates, or which day of the week is picked out by 'yesterday'.

'Contextualism' is the standard name for the view that words like 'know' and 'realize' are context-sensitive. Some of the appeal of contextualism comes from its promise to reconcile the main points in Chapters 1 and 2 of this book. Chapter 1 observed that the verb 'to know' is one of our most common verbs, and is used as the default label for ordinary cases of seeing, hearing, or remembering that something is the case. (Of course, you know that you are reading a book right now.) Chapter 2 observed that it's easy to discover ourselves doubting that knowledge is ever humanly possible. (How could you ever really know that you are reading a book and not just dreaming that this is so?) According to contextualists, there's no real clash between the positive remarks in the first chapter and the negative remarks in the second. Because 'know' is context-sensitive, everyday claims about how much you know are fully compatible with sceptical claims about your knowing almost nothing. The everyday speaker and the sceptic are in different conversational contexts, and are therefore saying different things when they use the word 'know'. Just as the sentence 'Tomorrow is Friday' sometimes says something true, and sometimes says something false (depending on when you say it), knowledge-ascribing sentences like 'John Doe knows that he is reading a book' do a similar trick. When everyday low standards are in force, it's right to say 'John Doe knows'; when we are using the sceptic's high standards, the thing to say is 'John Doe does not know.'

The emergence of contextualism

Contextualism grew out of a theory of knowledge launched in the early 1970s, the 'Relevant Alternatives' theory of knowledge. Advocates of that theory say that knowing always involves grasping some kind of contrast. Here's an example: Jane Roe is at the zoo with her son, and sees a black-and-white striped animal in the enclosure ahead of her. 'Look, Billy!' she says. 'That's a zebra!' She's right; there's nothing wrong with Jane's eyesight or her ability to recognize ordinary zoo animals, and the black-and-white striped animal she is looking at is indeed a zebra. When asked whether Jane Roe knows that the animal she is looking at is a zebra, we find it easy to say 'yes'. But here's a trickier question: does she know that the animal she is looking at is not *a cleverly disguised donkey*? (Figure 8). It's possible to paint stripes on a donkey and trim its ears and tail, and from where Jane is standing, a cleverly disguised donkey would look exactly the same to her. Jane Roe's evidence, according to the Relevant Alternatives theory, is good enough to enable her to tell that the animal is a zebra (as opposed to a lion, antelope, or camel). Given the range of animals at an ordinary zoo, she has a pretty easy set of relevant alternatives to pick from. However, her evidence is not good enough to enable her to tell that the animal is not a cleverly disguised donkey: to make that harder judgement, she'd have to rule out the relevant alternative that it actually *is* a cleverly disguised donkey. It is not impossible for her to rule out that tricky alternative, but Jane would need to hop the fence and go closer, perhaps even close enough to dab some cleansing fluid on the animal's fur. So, from 20 paces away, she knows that the animal is a zebra, but she doesn't know that the animal is not a cleverly disguised donkey.

In this example, it's understood that being a cleverly disguised donkey is not a relevant alternative at an ordinary zoo like the one Jane Roe is visiting, but it could be a relevant alternative at an impoverished zoo, or at a zoo run by practical jokers. One of the challenges facing the Relevant Alternatives theory is coming up

8. A cleverly disguised donkey

with the rules for setting what the relevant alternatives are for any given claim. The field of alternatives is partly set by what is actually possible for the speaker, but the further details of the theory have been hard to work out. Does it matter whether Jane Roe knows that the zoo is not run by jokers? It's unclear. But more importantly, there's something deeply *strange* about the Relevant Alternatives theory.

Let's assume that Jane knows some basic biology: suppose she knows, as most adults do, that zebras and donkeys are different species of animal, so that nothing can be both a zebra and a donkey

Box 6 A problem for the Relevant Alternatives theory of knowledge

What Jane knows from 20 paces away:

- That animal is a zebra.
- If that animal is a zebra, it is not a cleverly disguised donkey.

What she doesn't know:

- That animal is not a cleverly disguised donkey.

at the same time. If the animal is a zebra, then it follows from basic biology and logic that the animal is not a donkey. Logic also tells us that if something is not a donkey, it is not a cleverly disguised donkey. What the Relevant Alternatives theory says is that as Jane stands 20 paces away from the zebra, she knows that the animal she sees is a zebra, and also knows that if it is a zebra it is not a cleverly disguised donkey, but she doesn't know that the animal is not a cleverly disguised donkey. She can know the premises of the simple argument in Box 6 without being able to know the conclusion, despite being able to see for herself that it follows logically. The Relevant Alternatives theory therefore violates a principle called Closure, according to which you know anything that you succeed in deducing logically from your existing knowledge.

Violations of Closure seem weird: can't you trust logical deduction? Furthermore, as soon as we say that Jane doesn't know that the animal is not a cleverly disguised donkey, it sounds odd to insist she still knows it's a zebra. However, there is something compelling about the initial observations that motivated the Relevant Alternatives theory: it sounded right at first to describe Jane as knowing that the animal was a zebra, and it also sounded right to deny that she knew at a distance that the animal was not a donkey in disguise.

Contextualism emerged as a way of keeping the appealing part of the Relevant Alternatives Theory without accepting its strange denial of Closure. Published in 1976 by Gail Stine, the first clear formulation of contextualism was a two-part proposal. Stine's first claim was that we use higher or lower standards for knowledge in different settings: 'It is an essential characteristic of our concept of knowledge that tighter criteria are appropriate in different contexts. It is one thing in a street encounter, another in a classroom, another in a law court—and who is to say it cannot be another in a philosophical discussion?' Rather than having a field of alternatives fixed by what is possible for the person who is making the judgement, Stine proposed that various narrower or wider fields of alternatives are surveyed by those who are talking about whether a given person has knowledge. Stine's second point was to insist that within any given context, we appropriately stick to one set of standards. In a context in which we are worried about the possibility of doctored donkeys wearing make-up, it is wrong to say, 'Jane knows that the animal she is looking at is a zebra.' If she doesn't share our worries, Jane can truly say, 'I know that's a zebra,' but she can't then use pure logic and biology to deduce the exotic conclusion that it's not a cleverly disguised donkey. As soon as Jane starts thinking about cleverly disguised donkeys, her standards for knowledge will rise to take such exotic possibilities into account, and it will become wrong for her to say 'I know it's a zebra.' It's legitimate to talk about knowing with high standards or low standards; you just can't slide back and forth between the two in a single context without marking the shift.

In Stine's formulation of contextualism, knowing requires discrimination from a larger or smaller field of alternatives. The everyday speaker wonders whether the sandwich is chicken or tuna, and counts a person as knowing if he can rule one of those options out in favour of the other; the sceptic wonders about many more exotic alternatives as well (hypothetical new kinds of tuna that look like chicken, mere holograms of sandwiches, projections sent by an evil demon, and so forth). Once we have this wider array of alternatives to contend with, it's harder to credit anyone with knowledge. The widening and narrowing of a field of relevant alternatives is one vivid way in which contextualism can be expressed. But the basic idea behind contextualism is something more general, and not necessarily married to the relevant alternatives idea: the idea is that 'know' expresses something different as situations change, and different contextualist theories have different lines about how this works. There are internalist formulations of contextualism in which different contexts call for more or less evidence, and externalist formulations of contextualism in which belief-forming processes must track the truth across a narrower or broader array of circumstances as standards rise or fall. Contextualism on its own is not a theory of knowledge: it's a theory about knowledge-attributing language, a semantic topping that can be spread onto various different underlying theories of knowledge.

Is it an appetizing topping? Contextualism does promise a neat solution to the problem of scepticism: both sides are right, in a sense. The man in the street who says, 'I know that I am reading a book' is saying something true, but so is the sceptic who says, 'The man in the street does not know that he is holding a book.' The trick is that the word 'know' picks out a different relation for each of these speakers. Talking about scepticism raises the standards for knowledge, just as talking about basketball players raises the standards for 'tall', to use a favourite contextualist analogy. A man who measures six feet (183 cm) ordinarily counts as tall in the United States of America, where the average male height is about 5'9" (175 cm), even if six feet doesn't count as tall in the National Basketball Association, where the average height is about 6'7" (201 cm). Consider Chris Paul, a six-foot player for the LA Clippers. Sports fans discussing the strengths and weaknesses of the team can honestly say 'Chris Paul isn't tall' at the very moment that Chris Paul is honestly describing himself as tall on his dating website profile. There is no real conflict here, thanks to the difference in standards.

We have to be careful about speakers who are talking about what other speakers say: it would be a mistake for Chris to say 'What those sports fans said about me was false' simply on the basis of his being above average in height for an American man; it would also be a mistake for the fans to accuse Chris of saying something false on his dating profile simply on the basis of his being short for a professional basketball player. When you judge the truth or falsity of other speakers' context-sensitive remarks, you need to respect their context (and they need to do the same for you). The most straightforward thing to do would be to make the comparison class explicit. The sentence 'Chris Paul is tall' leaves a blank (compared to what?) that has to be filled in by context; both of the sentences 'Chris Paul is tall for an American man' and 'Chris Paul is not tall for a professional basketball player' have that blank filled in, and so express truths in a stable fashion across both contexts.

Going back to the case of knowledge, what's the clearest thing to say? Can we make our standards explicit? Is 'You know that you are reading a book' just like 'Chris Paul is tall'? If so, we should just be able to solve the problem of scepticism by saying something like 'You know, by low standards, that you are reading a book, but you don't know, by high standards, that you are reading a book.' Well, that was easy. But was it satisfying?

It's hard to say. Defending the context-sensitivity of 'know' isn't quite as smooth as defending the context-sensitivity of 'tall'. One objection that is often raised against contextualism is that it is really just scepticism in disguise. A sceptic doesn't have to fight the low-standards notion of knowledge in play in ordinary life; sceptics themselves doubtless use the verb 'know' dozens of times every day when they are talking to each other about ordinary things. What the sceptic really wants to say is that when we look closely and carefully at knowledge, we'll see that our everyday claims to have it are actually false. This doesn't amount to a call for stamping out all talk of knowledge, because we may succeed in communicating something useful in our casual talk about knowing. It could be interesting to hear a co-worker say, 'Lee knows who got the job,' for example. Thinking about the strict meaning of 'know', we may decide that Lee doesn't really know who got the job (could Lee really guarantee that he is right, and that the apparently successful candidate hasn't just been struck by a meteorite?). Maybe by saying 'Lee knows,' what's really communicated is that it's a good bet Lee could tell you. It's not crazy to think that you can convey something useful by saying something literally false: you use many words in this loose manner, like saying 'I'm starving,' when you are really just hungry. Even if that's literally false, it can help to get your host to offer you a snack. In the sceptic's high-standards context, 'Lee knows who got the job' expresses something false, even if we do something useful by saying that sentence in everyday contexts. But if contextualism says that sceptics speak truly when they deny that ordinary people know simple facts (like the fact that you are reading this book), then contextualism seems to be letting scepticism win, at the expense of common sense.

Contextualism is actually more subtle than the rough 'loose use' theory sketched above. In particular, contextualists are careful about respecting the context of other speakers. According to contextualism, sceptics get to say, truly, 'Lee doesn't know who got the job.' But they *don't* get to say that everyday speakers are saying something false when those everyday speakers say, 'Lee knows who got the job' in an everyday context. The same reasoning applies on the other side: ordinary people can express something true by saying, 'I know that I am reading a book,' in an ordinary context, but they cannot say that the sceptics are speaking falsely in saying, 'You don't know that you are reading a book' in the context of a high-standards philosophical discussion. Contextualists themselves don't have to say that the sceptical philosopher's context is better (or worse) than the common person's: high standards are not necessarily better than low standards (in fact, high standards can be really annoying and pedantic when you just want to send a card congratulating the person who got the job). Both sides win, as long as they play nice and refrain from putting down what the other side is saying.

Contextualism's tender tolerance for other points of view does not appeal to everyone. Critics of contextualism continue to resist the idea that the sceptic and the common man are both saying something true, and continue to wonder which way of talking *really* manages to get it right about knowledge itself, once and for all. From a contextualist perspective, asking which way of talking ultimately captures the nature of knowledge is like asking which weekday is ultimately 'tomorrow'. It's not a good question.

If contextualism aims to be somewhat friendly to both the sceptic and the common person, it has to be less friendly to the philosophical adversary who thinks there is a single true answer to the question 'Does Lee know who will get the job?' no matter which context we ask it in. That person really is making a mistake, contextualists will say, and they will say the same about anyone who thinks that the common person and the sceptic can't both speak truly. Contextualists do recognize that it's very common to think that one is forced to take sides: somehow the way in which 'know' is supposed to shift is more hidden from us than the way in which 'tall' or 'here' is. We don't have a big philosophical tradition of debates about which place is *really* 'here', in the way that we have debates about which way of talking is really right about knowledge. But why exactly would the context-sensitive workings of our language be obscured to us when we are talking about knowledge, if they are so transparent when we are talking about times, places, and qualities like 'tall'? One of the most active current research questions for contextualists concerns just this question, and various proposals have been advanced. Perhaps something about our use of 'know', like its role in closing off further enquiry, hampers us from tracking context shifts as well as we should, and gives us an illusion that knowledge is absolute. Or perhaps contextualism is wrong, and knowledge itself really is absolute. The view that knowledge is absolute, in the sense that the words we use for it are not context-sensitive, is known as 'invariantism'. Invariantism faces a challenge in explaining the shifting intuitions that make knowledge sometimes seem easy and sometimes seem hard.

Interest-relative invariantism

Lee is walking towards the bus stop after work when he bumps into his co-worker Smith, who is headed back into the building.

> —'Lee, do you know if the ground-floor supply room door is locked? I just realized I left my jacket in there, and I don't have a key.'
>
> —'Yes, it is—I know because I locked it myself half an hour ago, and I didn't see anyone else in that hallway after. Sorry!'

Lee doesn't seem to be saying anything controversial in claiming knowledge here, and we'll assume as we go forward that in fact the door really is locked, and that Lee's key, his eyesight, and his memory are all fine. But now we'll imagine a different version of the story, one that takes a different turn after Lee leaves the building. As Lee walks towards the bus stop, he is approached not by Smith, but by four police officers.

> —'Excuse me, sir, but we have an emergency situation in the building you just left. Apparently there was a shooting on the second floor, and the gunman is still in the building. Are there any ways out of the building other than the front door here?'
>
> —'There's a back door leading off the supply room, but I locked the door to that room half an hour ago.'
>
> —'Do you know if it's still locked, or if anyone else might have opened it?'
>
> —'I don't know—I didn't notice anyone go by, but I wasn't watching the door the whole time.'

In the forgotten-jacket version of the story, Lee claimed to know that the door was locked; in the gunman version, he claimed not to know. Both times he was saying something that sounded true. The curious thing is that both stories ran parallel up to the moment Lee left the building: in both stories he is trusting his memory of the last half hour as he answers the question about whether he knows. In traditional epistemology, whether or not you know depends on traditional factors such as whether your belief is true and how good your evidence is: interestingly enough, all these factors seem to be the same in both stories. So how is it possible that Lee knows the door is locked in the first, but doesn't know in the second?

It's clear what contextualists would say: in the casual bus-stop conversation, there are low standards in play, and when the police get involved, the standards rise. Lee is saying something true when he says 'I know' in the first story, but also when says 'I don't know' in the second. But this is not actually a story about how Lee knows in the first story and not in the second: it's a story about what a person can say truly in the two contexts. Viewed from other ('higher') perspectives, it would be *false* to say that Lee knew the door was locked in the first story, or so contextualism maintains. There is no simple, context-independent answer to the question 'Did Lee know or didn't he?'

If we were pushed towards contextualism by the feeling that it seems like Lee really does know in the first story, and doesn't in the second, then we might try to find a theory of knowledge which would fit those feelings more directly. If all the traditional factors that matter to epistemology (truth, evidence, reliability, and so forth) are the same in the two stories, one possibility is to allow some non-traditional factors to make a difference. What other factors are different in the two stories? Advocates of a position now known as interest-relative invariantism (IRI) have noticed that there are *practical* differences between the two stories. In the first, not much is at stake for Lee; as a friendly colleague he'll go back and unlock the door so Smith can get his jacket, but if he's wrong about the door still being locked, it's not a big problem. Finding it open would mean only that he'd wasted a minute on a short walk. In the second story, there could be serious practical consequences if Lee is wrong about the door being locked: the gunman could escape out the back exit.

Interest-relative invariantists have found that practical interests seem to have an impact in many cases. Do you know whether the sandwich is chicken or tuna? If not much is at stake (you like chicken just a little bit more, and you would slightly prefer to get soup instead if it's tuna), then a fairly casual inspection (looks like chicken) would be enough to count as knowing. If your life is at stake (you have a very serious fish allergy), then you will not know on the basis of that casual inspection, according to IRI. The more you have at stake, the more evidence you need in order to count as knowing. This is how the two versions of the Lee story can deliver different verdicts about whether Lee knows.

What makes IRI different from contextualism is that IRI is a theory about how knowledge itself works, not just a theory about the semantics of knowledge-ascribing vocabulary. The verdicts that it delivers are not just true-when-expressed-in-certain-contexts, but true full stop. Lee knows in the first story; he doesn't know in the second. The context that matters in setting the standards for how much evidence Lee needs for knowledge is Lee's own context, not the contexts of other people who might be talking about him from different perspectives. According to IRI, the sceptic is just wrong to say that Lee lacks knowledge in the first story. Different advocates of IRI have different accounts of the nature of knowledge; what they all have in common is that practical interests, which are not a factor for traditional epistemologists, are a factor that helps determine whether or not a person knows: as stakes rise, more evidence is needed for knowledge. Advocates of the theory contend that IRI is the best way of making sense of the relationship between knowledge and action.

Old-fashioned invariantism, again?

Contextualists were quick to criticize the IRI approach, noticing, for example, that it also has trouble capturing some patterns of shifting intuitions. If it's a plain context-independent fact that Lee knows that the door is locked in the first (forgotten-jacket) version of the story, how is it that the sceptic is able to make us start doubting that fact so easily? The IRI approach also gets awkward when we talk about counterfactual possibilities. 'The waiter doesn't know whether the sandwiches are tuna or chicken, but he would have known if it weren't for the fact that one of his customers has an allergy.' That sounds odd, but IRI predicts it shouldn't. Meanwhile, advocates of IRI have fired back at the contextualists, often by pointing out that 'know' doesn't really work like other context-sensitive vocabulary: unlike 'tall', it doesn't easily fit on a sliding scale, and unlike 'today', there are no simple rules for explaining how context fills it in. Contextualists have suggested that 'know' might have a special kind of context sensitivity all its own, but it's still an open question exactly how it works.

As the main shifting-standard views take shots at each other, advocates of more rigid standards have wondered whether their old-fashioned view might still win the day. Strict invariantists maintain that knowledge is determined strictly by traditional factors (truth, evidence, and the like) and that knowledge-attributing vocabulary is not sensitive to context. We've already met one of the most straightforward forms of strict invariantism: scepticism. According to Academic Scepticism, for example, there is a single fixed standard that must be met in order to have knowledge (we must have an infallibly correct impression of the thing judged). Sadly, we never meet this standard in daily life (or perhaps we meet it only for one or two special claims, like 'I exist'). If you take yourself to know you are reading a book, you are just wrong. Sceptics seem to owe us a story about why we speak so much of knowledge if it is forever out of reach, and we may or may not be satisfied with what they have to say. If we are unsatisfied, we may want to turn in the direction of moderate strict invariantism, which holds that there is a single fixed standard that must be met in order to have knowledge, but also that it is a standard that humans often meet. You do know that you are reading a book, and Lee really did know that the door was locked. Strict moderate invariantists also owe us something: they need to explain why exactly the sceptic can so easily lead us to doubt our everyday judgements, and why Lee's knowledge seemed to melt away as he was questioned by the police, even though the strictly traditional factors he was relying on remained the same. Strict moderate invariantists have struggled to answer these questions. One avenue they have tried is to argue that there is something wrong with our shifting intuitions, or with the cases that produce them. Perhaps the differences between the two versions of the locked-door story are larger than they seem: we assumed that the traditional factors that matter to knowledge were identical across those cases, but it's possible that the high stakes in one case will naturally trigger lower confidence or a different way of thinking about one's evidence. Or perhaps something about the high-stakes situation makes us confused about the difference between knowing and knowing that we know, or about the difference between what we are literally saying and what we are trying to convey. Perhaps there is something wrong with our instincts about these cases; perhaps some natural distortion is introduced when we talk to the sceptic or weigh life-and-death issues. Given how hard it is to develop a smooth story about our patterns of intuition about knowing, it makes sense to take a deeper look at how those intuitions are produced.

Chapter 8
Knowing about knowing

Epistemology's raw materials

How much do we know about knowledge before we start to study it systematically? We don't seem to start completely empty-handed. Philosophers have a special reason to hope that we have something at the outset, some talent for spotting genuine cases of knowledge: instincts or intuitions about particular cases are supposed to support some philosophical theories over others. If you felt that the person looking at the broken clock didn't know the time, that feeling was taken to work as a reason for you to reject the classical analysis of knowledge. But what enabled you to judge that case the way you did? And can you tell whether your way of judging—whether or not others share it—is really getting it right? These questions have recently sparked fresh empirical and philosophical work on our intuitions about knowledge.

Reading minds

The word 'intuition' may suggest some mystical power of insight, but intuitions about knowledge are a feature of everyday life. Focus for a moment on the difference between these two claims: (1) 'Lee thinks that he is being followed.' (2) 'Lee knows that he is being followed.' There's a significant difference here, but the choice to say one thing rather than the other doesn't usually involve deliberate calculation. You can feel that someone knows something (or doesn't know it) without calling to mind any explicit theory of knowledge: this kind of feeling is an intuition. There's a name for the natural capacity that generates instinctive feelings about knowledge and other mental states: mindreading. The word is popularly used for stage magic acts in which a magician performs an impossible-seeming trick of reading another person's thoughts. As psychologists use the term, it applies to something that we do a hundred times a day with no special fanfare. Mindreading is the attribution of 'hidden' or underlying mental states—wanting, fearing, thinking, knowing, hoping, and the rest—to another person. When you see someone reach towards something, you do not simply have the impression that an arm is extending in space; you see the person as reaching for the salt, wanting something, and aiming to get it. As we register, perhaps only subconsciously, which way people are reaching and glancing, and as we detect tiny shifts in their facial expressions, we gain a sense of what is going on inside them and how well they grasp their environment, and we become better able to predict how they will act and interact with us. Without a capacity for mindreading, we'd be stuck looking at surface patterns of moving limbs and facial features; mindreading gives us access to deeper states within a person. Whether we are trying to coordinate or compete with others, it helps enormously to know what they want and know, and whether they are friendly, angry, or impatient. We don't always get it right: it's possible to mistake what someone knows or wants, or to be misled by a skilled deceiver, but our daily social navigation is so effective that it comes as a surprise when we occasionally misread a situation.

The mindreading abilities of human beings are better than those of any other species on earth. Chimpanzees monitor whether their rivals do or do not know about hidden food: they grasp the simple contrast between having and lacking knowledge. But human beings can also keep track of the ways in which others are mistaken, and this is something that no other animal does (as far as we can tell). You can see another person as having a false belief: playing a practical joke on a friend, you empty his cereal box and fill it with rubber insects. You know, as you watch him sitting down at the breakfast table, that he is expecting cereal to pour from the box. You know that he has an inner representation that doesn't match the actual outer reality. No other animal seems to be capable of representing this kind of state, even in situations in which it would be highly advantageous. In experimental tests of whether an animal can keep track of another's false belief, all non-human animals fail.

These tests are hard enough that human beings fail too, at least when they are toddlers. Here's one of the classic demonstrations of this failure: a young child is given a familiar container, such as a candy box with a picture of candy on it, and asked what is inside. ('Candy!') Then there's a surprise: the box is opened to reveal that it contains not candy, but crayons. The box is closed again, and the child is then asked what the next child, waiting outside, will think when she comes into the room. Will that child know what is in the closed box? What will she think is in the box? Almost all five-year-olds recognize that the next child will have a false belief about the contents of the box, but only a small minority of three-year-olds can get this right. Strangely enough, most three-year-olds say that the next child will already know that there are crayons in the box, and even more strangely, many three-year-olds give the wrong answer when they are asked what they themselves thought at first on seeing the box. Calculating another person's false belief is a demanding task, as is remembering your own past mistake: you have to suppress your current picture of how the world is in order to depict things from the mistaken person's point of view. Belief or opinion, a state which may or may not match the outer world, is a relatively tricky state to represent. If knowledge is a state that must reflect how things are, then the attribution of knowledge is simpler.

Advocates of the 'knowledge first' programme in epistemology have claimed support for their position from these findings and from various other lines of research supporting the notion that states of knowledge are easier to represent than states of mere belief. For example, across cultures, the verb 'know' is acquired earlier and used more heavily than the verb 'think'. Critics have argued that the order in which we learn these concepts may not reveal which of them is really basic: after all, we learn about table salt well before we learn about the elements that make it up, and we also talk about the compound more often. Critics have also raised questions about whether children too young to grasp the concept of false belief can already be credited with the concept of knowledge. To complicate matters further, recent research suggests that young children and even infants do have some partial and implicit capacity to recognize false beliefs, although the scope and significance of this capacity are still unclear. We are still struggling to figure out the true developmental story about the human ability to spot knowledge, but continuing research into this difficult territory can still give us a clearer picture of the natural structure of our everyday concepts of knowledge and belief.

More broadly, empirical work can also give us a better sense of the natural limits of our powers of mindreading. These powers involve some very specialized equipment. You can flex this equipment by reading the three very short stories in Box 7, used in research led by MIT neuroscientist Rebecca Saxe.

As you were reading these stories, different regions of your brain were selectively activated. Young children's brains don't respond very differently to the second and third stories, but for older children and adults, the third story is quite distinctive. To understand it, you need to represent the characters' states of mind. Reading stories like this selectively activates a brain region near your right ear: the right temporo-parietal junction (RTPJ). Other regions are involved as well, including the medial prefrontal cortex (MPFC), which is activated in adults and children by all kinds of stories about people, including the second story above. The RTPJ is also activated in young children for all stories with social content,

Box 7 Stories that activate different brain regions

1. Physical

Out behind the big red barn at the edge of the walnut grove is the most magnificent pond in the neighbourhood. It is wide and deep, and shaded by an old oak tree. There are all sorts of things in that pond: fish and old shoes and lost toys and tricycles, and many other surprises.

2. People

Old Mr McFeeglebee is a grey wrinkled old farmer, who wears grey wrinkled old overalls, and grey wrinkled old boots. He has lived on this land his whole life, longer even than most of the trees. Little Georgie is Mr McFeeglebee's nephew from town.

3. Mental

Mr McFeeglebee doesn't want any little boys to fish in the ponds. But little Georgie pretends not to notice. He likes fishing so much, and besides, he knows he can run faster than anybody in town. Georgie decides to run away really fast if Mr McFeeglebee sees him fishing.

but the mature RTPJ responds in particular to stories about what people know, want, decide, pretend, believe, and so forth. When this section of the brain is damaged by a stroke or lesion (or temporarily disabled in an experiment, through transcranial magnetic stimulation), we become deeply impaired in our ability to evaluate and predict what others know and what they will do.

It's not surprising that mindreading comes to have its own specialized area in the adult brain: although we can do it effortlessly, mindreading involves some complex calculations. In this respect it has something in common with face recognition, which also involves very rapid and effortless calculations, and is also highly specialized within one specific area of the adult brain. What is the relationship between what someone wants, notices, pretends, and plans to do when he is seen? Navigating around these patterns is a non-trivial task. If we are able to decide, in the course of a casual conversation, whether to describe someone as just thinking or really knowing something, we can do this without conscious calculation in part because we have specialized brain resources devoted to the task of tracking mental states.

There are natural limitations to our mindreading equipment. One limit is a simple capacity limit on how many nested levels of mental state we can represent. Here's a sentence which uses four levels: 'Davis thinks that Lee knows that Smith doesn't want Jones to find out about the job.' Did you follow that? Researchers have tested people on their capacity to track up to nine levels, but most adults can manage only five levels before they break down and start to answer comprehension questions randomly (people with larger social circles do a bit better). This limitation is like our limitation in tracking moving objects on a screen (most people can manage five, heavy video gamers can go a bit higher): we have only so much attention to go around.

Here's a deeper limitation that is specific to mindreading: we have a tendency to be self-centred. More precisely, we suffer from a bias called 'egocentrism', which makes it difficult for us to override our own perspective when we are evaluating others who know less about their situation than we do. The bias is very pronounced in young children: the candy-box task described above is one example. A young child who knows that there are crayons in the box has trouble imagining that others could fail to know this. Children also have trouble recognizing the limits of others' informational access to the world. For example, having lifted a pair of visually identical piggy banks, one light and one heavy, even older children able to pass the candy-box task will wrongly predict that someone who just sees the two piggy banks from a distance will be able to tell which is the heavy one.

Even adults still make errors along the same lines. It remains difficult to bracket our own private knowledge of a situation when calculating the perspective of someone more naive. For example, in stock-trading games where one side is given special 'insider' information that they know the other side lacks, the better-informed side has trouble setting aside what they know in calculating how the other side will respond to offers, even when it would be really advantageous to calculate the naive view accurately. It's also tough to suppress our own private knowledge of a situation when we are evaluating how well or poorly someone has been thinking in making a decision: if you are told that a long-odds gamble ended up working out favourably, that information will colour your assessment of the wisdom of the gambler to a much larger extent than you might expect, even if you recognize that it is unreasonable on your part to take that outcome information into account.

It's not entirely clear why we have so much trouble subtracting from our own special knowledge when trying to represent or evaluate other perspectives, but we do know that the egocentric bias is very robust: some biases can be suppressed if you forewarn people about them, or if you give cash incentives for better performance, but egocentrism sticks with us even under those conditions. Epistemologists have wondered whether this limitation on our natural capacity to see other perspectives could be playing some role in the pattern of intuitions motivating contextualism. Once I am thinking about tricky alternatives like disguised donkeys, I will have trouble evaluating the perspective of a naive zoo visitor: even if I'm explicitly aware that she isn't thinking about those strange possibilities, egocentrism can drive me to evaluate her as though she is. Whether or not this works as a strategy for explaining the intuitions behind contextualism, epistemologists can profit from a better understanding of the natural mechanisms behind our intuitions about the presence and absence of knowledge. If some intuitions can be shown to arise from natural limitations or biases in our mindreading capacity, we can handle them with special caution as we construct our theories of knowledge.

Challenges to the case method

Philosophers interested in the nature of our intuitions can look at empirical work on mindreading, but they can also try something much more direct: polling ordinary people about their intuitions on the cases that matter to epistemology. Known as experimental philosophy, this method turned up some surprising results, especially in its early days. One of the first published papers in experimental philosophy, a 2001 paper by Jonathan Weinberg and colleagues, investigated responses to a series of vignettes about people making judgements. Some of the cases were easy: does a person who has a 'special feeling' that a coin will land heads actually know that it will? (over 90 per cent said 'no'). Some of the

Box 8 Weinberg and Colleagues' American Car case (2001)

Bob has a friend, Jill, who has driven a Buick for many years. Bob therefore thinks that Jill drives an American car. He is not aware, however, that her Buick has recently been stolen, and he is also not aware that Jill has replaced it with a Pontiac, which is a different kind of American car. Does Bob really know that Jill drives an American car, or does he only believe it?

Circle one:

REALLY KNOWS   ONLY BELIEVES

cases were hard, involving complicated hypothetical conspiracies. One of the harder cases (featured in Box 8) was a Gettier-type story. An overall majority of the experimental participants reported that the central character in the case lacked knowledge, judging the case in the same way that mainstream philosophers would. But not every subgroup performed the same way: while 74 per cent of the 66 participants who self-identified as 'Western' gave the standard answer, only 43 per cent of the 23 self-identified 'East Asian' participants and 39 per cent of the 23 'Indian Subcontinental' participants did so. Weinberg and colleagues concluded that philosophers who trust their intuitions in epistemology are not discovering the objective nature of knowledge but rather are engaged in the quite different activity of revealing their own local cultural attitudes, attitudes which might not be shared by other groups, and need not show us anything about the nature of knowledge itself. The experimental philosophy movement advocated abandoning the use of intuitions in philosophy.

Traditional philosophers were annoyed. Some of them objected to details of the case: its subject matter—American car brands—could interest some groups more than others, and the story is more readable to those who recognize at once that a Buick is an American car. Furthermore, the story is open to being fleshed out in different ways: are we supposed to think of Jill as the kind of person who just always drives an American car, and could her friend Bob know this fact about her? If we think of the story that way, it's not even a Gettier case: the theft of the Buick doesn't destroy the long-standing tendency of Jill's that is known to her friend. Other philosophers argued that we can't place too much stock in the quick responses of amateurs, which are doubtless influenced by all kinds of random factors: intuitions about philosophical scenarios only count if they are the products of careful reflection. Caution is needed in pushing that last line, however, at least among philosophers who claim that they are developing theories to make sense of pre-theoretical intuitions. If you have to think really hard about what your intuition is on a case, critics charged, your theory might be contaminating your judgement.

Later research challenged Weinberg's original findings while leaving some of experimental philosophy's larger questions in place. More systematic investigations of a wider variety of cases have failed to show that there is anything peculiarly Western about the intuitions traditionally reported by philosophers. Larger studies involving many participants from different cultures have in fact shown quite consistent patterns of knowledge attribution, across men and women of different cultures, for various Gettier cases, including the original 'American Car' story. Ordinary people do tend to agree with professional philosophers in judging that the agents in Gettier-type cases lack knowledge. Where Weinberg and colleagues were concerned that Gettier responses arose only from a very particular cultural group, and couldn't therefore be taken as evidence about knowledge itself, subsequent work favours the notion that these responses are universal. These more recent findings fit with cross-cultural work on the development of the concept of knowledge. Children in large urban pre-schools in London and Toyko go through the same broad sequence of stages in separating knowledge from ignorance and from false belief as children in rural hunter-gatherer societies in Cameroon. To be sure, adult performance is sometimes different across cultures—for example, Chinese adults seem to outperform American adults in the speed and accuracy of certain computations of other points of view—but the underlying competence to spot knowledge seems to be the same across cultures. If early work in experimental philosophy raised the worry that philosophers had peculiar intuitions about knowledge not shared by others, more recent work seems to be putting those worries to rest. Deeper worries remain, however. The fact that an impression is broadly shared is not always a sign that this impression is right.

Just as ordinary people share professional philosophers' intuitions about Gettier cases, they share their intuitions about some more problematic cases. Imagine a man called Albert in an ordinary furniture store. Albert sees a bright red table that he likes, checks the price, and asks his wife, 'Do you like this red table?' Thinking about the case, would you say that Albert knows that the table is red? (Of students polled in a recent study, 92 per cent said 'yes'.) Now consider a version of the story that just adds a few more details. The table is indeed red, and the lighting in the store is normal. But we will draw your attention to a further fact: if it were a white table under a bright red spotlight, it would look *exactly the same* to Albert, and Albert *has not checked whether the lighting is in fact normal*. Does Albert know that the table is red? (Suddenly less than half of the survey participants say 'yes'.) For some reason, thinking about a possibility of error, even when it's clear that Albert is not at risk of making that error, greatly reduces people's inclination to see Albert as knowing. Notice that the two stories weren't about two characters in objectively different settings; the second story just added some details that could also have been stated in the first version as well. It's as if we shifted from being generous about knowledge to being stingy when we thought about the case harder. This is the pattern of intuitions that has driven some philosophers towards scepticism and pushed others towards contextualism.

On the surface, there is an inconsistency between the two judgements. Sceptics think that only our second intuition (that Albert lacks knowledge) can be trusted; after all, that's the intuition we had when we thought harder about the situation. Contextualists think that the apparent inconsistency isn't a real inconsistency: both intuitions are fine, and they don't even really clash, because we meant something tougher by 'knows' in the second case, when we were thinking about tricky possibilities. Albert met the low standard but not the high one, just as a man could be tall for an American but not tall for a professional basketball player. Meanwhile, moderate invariantists think that

9. The Hermann Grid illusion

he second, more sceptical, intuition is the one that's mistaken,
perhaps arising from some psychological bias. For example, we
could be evaluating Albert as if he himself is thinking about the
possibility of tricky lighting but perversely refusing to check
whether the lighting is normal before he makes up his mind that
he table is red. According to the moderate invariantist view,
our response to this case is a cognitive illusion: something in the
brain naturally miscalculates here, the same way the eye naturally
miscalculates the shading of the spots at the corners of the boxes
n the Hermann Grid illusion (Figure 9). Work in experimental
philosophy now shows that this pattern of intuitions is widely
shared, but it still doesn't tell us which of the intuitions in
he pattern are really capturing the nature of knowledge, and

which intuitions, if any, are illusory. How can we resolve this problem?

Impressions of knowledge, and knowledge itself

Some philosophers have argued that our situation here is hopeless. You can check whether your wristwatch is running fast or slow by comparing it to the National Research Council atomic clock, but there's no obvious counterpart for checking the accuracy of your intuitions about knowledge. If you've had trouble coming up with a smooth theory of knowledge that explains all of your instinctive feelings about particular cases, you may suspect that some of these feelings are illusions. But which ones? Philosopher Robert Cummins contends that we could only sort out which intuitions about knowledge were the right ones if we had some independent intuition-free access to the nature of knowledge itself. But if we had that kind of direct access we wouldn't have to fumble with intuitions about particular cases to grasp the nature of knowledge: 'If you know enough to start fixing problems with philosophical intuition, you already know enough to get along without it.' Cummins concludes that philosophers should never rely on intuitions about cases in formulating theories of knowledge.

That's a very pessimistic response. The parallel move in the perceptual domain would be to say that we can't start fixing problems with our visual impressions of colour, and figuring out which ones are illusory, until we have an independent, vision-free way of accessing colour. Although we are starting to develop technologies that can sort out colour signals without reliance on the human eye—photometers can measure the colours on that diagram of the Hermann Grid and won't get confused about the corner spots—we didn't actually wait until we had that equipment to start sorting out the illusions from the accurate impressions. We have used a variety of techniques over time to figure out which impressions are right, including double-checking impressions in different contexts or from different angles. Our understanding of

10. Can we make progress?

vision has evolved alongside our understanding of the nature of light and colour.

Meanwhile, even without the epistemological equivalent of a photometer to detect states of knowledge, our investigation of intuitions about knowledge can also evolve alongside our investigation of knowledge itself. As we move towards a better understanding of our knowledge-spotting instincts, fitting them into a broader picture of our psychology, we become better able to sort out which intuitions should count. Meanwhile, a sharper philosophical picture of knowledge itself will help advance our understanding of the nature of those instincts. Tools other than intuitions can also be used to tackle the problem of knowledge. We can work to develop internally consistent theories of knowledge that fit with our broader theories of human language, logic, science, and learning. We can refine our rough intuitive sense of the conditions that make knowledge possible by building mathematical models of individual and group knowledge. We can compare the strengths of existing philosophical theories generated in a range of historical periods and across different cultures. Some philosophical claims about knowledge have turned out to be confused or self-undermining, but other findings about knowledge, like its special connection with truth, have stood the test of time. If we do not know in advance which of our methods will be best suited to deliver further insight into the nature of knowledge, this is in part because we still do not fully understand what knowledge is. But even if we have yet to secure full knowledge of the nature of knowledge, we now find ourselves in a better position to make progress on this ancient question.

References

Chapter 1: Introduction

Data on the frequency of 'know' and 'think' in English are from *Word Frequencies in Written and Spoken English*, by Geoffrey Leech, Paul Rayson, and Andrew Wilson (New York: Routledge, 2001). For other languages, see the Linguistic Data Consortium website (<http://www.ldc.upenn.edu/>).

The claim that 'know' is a linguistic universal is defended by Anna Wierzbicka in her *Semantics: Primes and Universals* (New York: Oxford University Press, 1996).

The observations about verbs of ingestion and motion, and the examples in Box 1, are from Cliff Goddard's 'Universals and Variation in the Lexicon of Mental State Concepts', in *Words and the Mind: How Words Capture Human Experience* (New York: Oxford University Press, 2010).

The classic treatment of the factivity of 'knows' is Paul Kiparsky and Carol Kiparsky's paper 'Fact', in M. Bierwisch and K. Heidolph (eds), *Progress in Linguistics* (The Hague: Mouton, 1970). There is also a helpful discussion of factivity in the first chapter of Timothy Williamson's *Knowledge and its Limits* (Oxford: Oxford University Press, 2000).

The explanation of the projected use of 'knows' is drawn from Richard Holton's paper 'Some Telling Examples', *Journal of Pragmatics*, 28 (1997): 625–8.

Protagoras's relativism is discussed in Plato's dialogue *Theaetetus. The Theaetetus of Plato*. Trans. M. J. Levett, ed. Myles Burnyeat (Indianapolis: Hackett Publishing Company, 1990).

Chapter 2: Scepticism

The quotations from Sextus are from pp. 48–9 of Julia Annas and Jonathan Barnes's edition of *Sextus Empiricus: The Outlines of Scepticism* (Cambridge: Cambridge University Press, 2000).

The quotation from Śrīharśa's *The Sweets of Refutation* is from Ganganatha Jha's translation, 2nd edition (Delhi: Sri Satguru Publications, 1986), p. 3.

The quotation from Descartes is from Cottingham, Stoothoff, and Murdoch (trans.), *The Philosophical Writings of Descartes*, Vol. II (Cambridge: Cambridge University Press, 1984), p. 374.

The quotations from G. E. Moore are from pp. 295, 296, and 300 of 'Proof of An External World', *Proceedings of the British Academy*, 25 (1939): 273–300.

Bertrand Russell's views on scepticism are explained in *The Problems of Philosophy* (London: Williams & Norgate, 1912).

Jonathan Vogel's spatial structure argument is from 'The Refutation of Scepticism', in Mattias Steup and Ernest Sosa (eds), *Contemporary Debates in Epistemology* (Oxford: Blackwell, 2005), pp. 72–84.

The most influential statement of semantic externalism is Saul Kripke's *Naming and Necessity* (Cambridge, MA: Harvard University Press, 1973). Putnam uses semantic externalism against scepticism in *Reason, Truth and History* (Cambridge: Cambridge University Press, 1981).The 'fledgling brain-in-a-vat' objection was raised by Anthony Brueckner, 1986, 'Brains in a Vat', *Journal of Philosophy*, 83(3): 148–67.

David Chalmers's essay 'The Matrix as Metaphysics' was published in *Philosophers Explore the Matrix* (New York: Oxford University Press, 2005), pp. 132–76.

Timothy Williamson draws the immune system analogy in 'Knowledge and Scepticism', in Frank Jackson and Michael Smith (eds), *The Oxford Handbook of Contemporary Philosophy* (New York: Oxford University Press, 2005), pp. 681–700.

Chapter 3: Rationalism and empiricism

The quotation from Paracelsus is from Jolande Jacobi and Norbert Guterman's *Paracelsus: Selected Writings* (Princeton: Princeton University Press, 1995), pp. 112–14.

Francesco Sizzi's claims about Jupiter are made on pp. 16–17 of his treatise *Understanding Astronomy, Optics and Physics* (Venice: 1611).

Montaigne advocates that we should not take sides between the earth-centred and the sun-centred models in his essay 'An Apology for Raymond Sébond', in *The Complete Essays of Montaigne*, trans. M. A. Screech (New York: Penguin, 1987), p. 642.

The quotations from Descartes are from volume II, pp. 4 and 12 of Cottingham, Stoothoff, and Murdoch's translation of *The Philosophical Writings of Descartes* (Cambridge: Cambridge University Press, 1984).

The quotations from Locke are from the following books, chapters, and sections of his *Essay Concerning Human Understanding*: 1.1.3, 4.7.9, 1.2.5, 4.3.18, 4.1.2, 4.2.14. P. H. Nidditch (ed.) (Oxford: Oxford University Press, 1979).

Chapter 4: The analysis of knowledge

Russell tells the clock story in *Human Knowledge: Its Scope and Limits* (London: Allen and Unwin, 1948), pp. 170–1.

Edmund Gettier's paper 'Is Justified True Belief Knowledge?' was published in *Analysis*, 23 (6) (1963): 121–3.

The no-false-belief rule was advocated by Michael Clark, 'Knowledge and Grounds: A Comment on Mr. Gettier's Paper', *Analysis*, 24 (2) (1963): 46–8. The objection that Clark's proposal would rule out clear cases of knowledge was pressed by John Turk Saunders and Naratan Champawat, 'Mr. Clark's Definition of "Knowledge"', *Analysis*, 25 (1) (1964): 8–9.

William Lycan argues for the rule that knowledge must not be essentially based on any false assumptions in 'On the Gettier Problem Problem', in Stephen Hetherington (ed.), *Epistemology Futures* (Oxford: Oxford University Press, 2006), pp. 148–68; against this proposal, see Ted Warfield, 'Knowledge from Falsehood', *Philosophical Perspectives*, 19 (1) (2005): 405–16, and Branden Fitelson, 'Strengthening the Case for Knowledge from Falsehood', *Analysis*, 70 (4) (2010): 666–9.

Alvin Goldman proposed the causal theory of knowledge in 'A Causal Theory of Knowing', *Journal of Philosophy*, 64 (12) (1967): 357–72. He formulates reliabilism in 'Discrimination and Perceptual Knowledge', *Journal of Philosophy*, 73 (20) (1976): 771–91.

The lottery objection to reliabilism is pressed by John Hawthorne in his book *Knowledge and Lotteries* (Oxford: Oxford University Press, 2004).

Linda Zagzebski's recipe for creating Gettier cases is in 'The Inescapability of Gettier Problems', *Philosophical Quarterly*, 44 (174) (1994): 65–73.

Matt Weiner argues that our use of 'know' is guided by inconsistent principles in 'The (Mostly Harmless) Inconsistency of Knowledge Ascriptions', *Philosophers' Imprint*, 9 (1) (2009): 1–25. Mark Kaplan argues that epistemology should focus on justification rather than knowledge in 'It's Not What You Know that Counts', *The Journal of Philosophy*, 82 (7) (1985): 350–63.

Timothy Williamson advocates abandoning the programme of analysis in Chapter 1 of *Knowledge and its Limits* (Oxford: Oxford University Press, 2000). The quotation is from p. 47.

The Ancient Gettier cases are drawn from Dharmottara's *Ascertainment of Knowledge* (*c.*770 CE). The 'distant fire' case follows Jonathan Stoltz's rendition in 'Gettier and Factivity in Indo-Tibetan Epistemology', *Philosophical Quarterly*, 57 (228) (2007): 394–415, and the 'desert mirage' case is drawn from Georges Dreyfus's presentation of it in *Recognizing Reality: Dharmakīrti's Philosophy and its Tibetan interpretations* (Albany: SUNY Press, 1997).

Gaṅgeśa's causal theory of knowledge is laid out in the perception chapter of his *Jewel of Reflection on the Truth about Epistemology*, Stephen Phillips and Ramanuja Tatacharya (trans.) (New York: American Institute of Buddhist Studies, 2004).

Chapter 5: Internalism and externalism

Nozick's tracking theory of knowledge is laid out in his *Philosophical Explanations* (Cambridge, MA: Harvard University Press, 1981).

Goldman acknowledges the problem of individuating belief-forming processes in 'Discrimination and Perceptual Knowledge', *The Journal of Philosophy*, 73 (20) (1976): 771–91; the problem is pressed against reliabilism by Earl Conee and Richard Feldman in 'The Generality Problem for Reliabilism', *Philosophical Studies*, 89.1 (1998): 1–29.

Juan Comesaña argues that, due to considerations of basing, the Generality Problem is everyone's problem, in 'A Well-Founded Solution to the Generality Problem', *Philosophical Studies*, 129.1 (2006): 27–47.

BonJour's Samantha example is from 'Externalist Theories of
  Empirical Knowledge', *Midwest Studies in Philosophy*, 5 (1)
  (1980): 53–74. BonJour lays out his objections to the idea of
  rescuing externalism by adding an internalist 'no-defeater' clause
  in *Epistemic Justification: Internalism vs. Externalism,
  Foundations vs. Virtues* (Malden, MA: Wiley-Blackwell, 2003).
The division between automatic and systematic thinking is explained
  in Jonathan Evans's *Thinking Twice: Two Minds in One Brain*
  (Oxford: Oxford University Press, 2010).

Chapter 6: Testimony

Locke's story about the King of Siam is from 4.15.5 of the *Essay
  Concerning Human Understanding*, and the checklist for
  determining the rational degree of confidence in testimony is from
  4.15.4.
Dan Sperber discusses bees and people in 'An Evolutionary perspective
  on testimony and argumentation', *Philosophical Topics*, 29 (2001):
  401–13. Ruth Millikan defends the view that even human
  testimonial knowledge transmission is 'cognition by proxy' in
  Language, Thought and Other Biological Categories (Cambridge:
  MIT Press, 1984).
The concept of 'Epistemic Vigilance' is explained in a paper of that
  title by Dan Sperber, Fabrice Clement, Christophe Heintz, Olivier
  Mascaro, Hugo Mercier, Gloria Origgi, and Deirdre Wilson, *Mind
  & Language*, 25 (4) (2010): 359–93.
The discussion of Gautama is based on Chapter 6 of Stephen Phillips's
  Epistemology in Classical India (Routledge 2012); the quotation
  (from an ancient commentary on Gautama) is from the *Nyāya-
  Sūtra* ed. A.M. Tarkatirtha, Taranatha Nyayatarkatirtha, and
  H. K. Tarkatirtha, 1936–45 (rpt.1985), as quoted by Phillips at
  p. 83 of *Epistemology in Classical India*.
The story of the lawyer is from *The Theaetetus of Plato*. Trans.
  M. J. Levett, ed. Myles Burnyeat (Indianapolis: Hackett Publishing
  Company, 1990), p. 338.
The quotation from Jennifer Lackey is from *Learning from Words*,
  (New York: Oxford University Press), p. 47.
The reliability of Wikipedia articles is reviewed in Jim Giles, 'Internet
  encyclopaedias go head to head', *Nature*, 438 (7070) (2005):
  900–1.

Edward Craig's position on testimony is explained in his book
Knowledge and the State of Nature (Oxford: Clarendon Press, 1990).

Chimpanzees' failure to distinguish between knowledgeable and
ignorant informants is documented in Daniel Povinelli, Alyssa Rulf,
and Donna Bierschwale's 'Absence of knowledge attribution and
self-recognition in young chimpanzees', *Journal of Comparative
Psychology* 108 (1) (1994): 74–80. Their ability to track what
competitors know is described in Hare, B., Call, J., and Tomasello, M.
(2001), 'Do chimpanzees know what conspecifics know?' *Animal
Behaviour* 61 (1): 139–51.

Chapter 7: Shifting standards?

On the semantics of words like 'tall', see Peter Ludlow's 'Implicit
Comparison Classes', *Linguistics and Philosophy*, 12 (1989):
519–33.

The Relevant Alternatives theory was advanced by Fred Dretske in
'Epistemic Operators', *Journal of Philosophy*, 64 (24) (1970):
1007–23.

Gail Stine introduces contextualism in 'Skepticism, Relevant
Alternatives, and Deductive Closure', *Philosophical Studies*, 29 (4)
(1976): 249–61. The quotation is from p. 254.

Stewart Cohen presents an internalist, evidence-centred version of
contextualism in 'Contextualism, Skepticism, and the Structure
of Reasons', *Philosophical Perspectives*, 13 (1999): 57–89; for
externalist versions of contextualism, see David Lewis, 'Elusive
Knowledge', *Australasian Journal of Philosophy*, 74 (1996):
549–67 and Keith DeRose, *The Case for Contextualism*, volume I
(Oxford: Oxford University Press, 2009).

The point about respecting other speakers' contexts is made most
clearly by Keith DeRose in 'Contextualism and Knowledge
Attributions', *Philosophy and Phenomenological Research*, 52
(1992): 913–29. DeRose applies contextualism to the sceptical
problem in 'Solving the Skeptical Problem', *The Philosophical
Review*, 104 (1995): 1–52.

'Interest-relative invariantism' is a label coined by Jason Stanley; he
defends the position in his book *Knowledge and Practical Interests*
(Oxford: Oxford University Press, 2005).

Keith DeRose defends the idea that 'know(s)' could have its own kind
of context-sensitivity in *The Case for Contextualism*, volume I

(Oxford: Oxford University Press, 2009); he also observes that IRI has trouble accounting for certain common patterns of intuition.

Timothy Williamson argues that contextualism misdiagnoses cases in which we are actually confused about the difference between knowing and knowing that we know, in 'Contextualism, subject-sensitive invariantism and knowledge of knowledge', *Philosophical Quarterly*, 55 (2005): 213–35. Patrick Rysiew argues that contextualists are mistaken about the pragmatics of knowledge attributions in 'The Context-Sensitivity of Knowledge Attributions', *Noûs* 35 (4) (2001): 477–514.

Chapter 8: Knowing about knowing

On primate inability to represent false belief even in competitive situations, see Juliane Kaminski, Josep Call, and Michael Tomasello, 'Chimpanzees know what others know, but not what they believe', *Cognition*, 109 (2) (2008): 224–34.

The hidden contents task is from Juergen Hogrefe, Heinz Wimmer and Josef Perner, 'Ignorance versus false belief: A developmental lag in attribution of epistemic states', *Child Development*, 57 (3) (1986): 567–82.

For a debate over the significance of developmental and comparative psychology to the knowledge-first programme, see Jennifer Nagel, 'Knowledge as a Mental State', and the replies to it, by Patrick Rysiew, Stephen Butterfill, and Johannes Roessler, in *Oxford Studies in Epistemology*, 4 (2012): 273–344.

Work on the early infant implicit recognition of false belief starts with Kristine Onishi and Renée Baillargeon, 'Do 15-month-old infants understand false beliefs?' *Science*, 308 (5719) (2005): 255–8. For discussion of some lingering questions about early infant mindreading, see Celia Heyes, 'False Belief in Infancy: A fresh look', *Developmental Science* (2014).

The short stories in Box 7 are from Rebecca Saxe, Susan Whitfield-Gabrieli, Jonathan Scholz, and Kevin Pelphrey, 'Brain Regions for Perceiving and Reasoning about Other People in School-Aged Children', *Child Development*, 80 (4) (2009): 1197–209. The role of the RTPJ in mindreading is explained in Rebecca Saxe and Nancy Kanwisher, 'People thinking about thinking people: the role of the temporo-parietal junction in the theory of mind', *Neuroimage*, 19 (2003): 1835–42.

Observations on the limits of nested mental state attribution are from Peter Kinderman, Robin Dunbar, and Richard P. Bentall's 'Theory-of-mind deficits and causal attributions', *British Journal of Psychology*, 89, no. 2 (1998): 191–204. On those with larger social circles doing better, see James Stiller and Robin Dunbar, 'Perspective-taking and memory capacity predict social network size', *Social Networks*, 29 (1) (2007): 93–104.

On the limits of the number of objects we can track at a time, see Zenon Pylyshyn and Ron Storm, 'Tracking multiple independent targets: Evidence for a parallel tracking mechanism', *Spatial Vision*, 3 (3) (1988): 179–97.

On egocentrism, see Susan Birch and Paul Bloom, 'Understanding children's and adults' limitations in mental state reasoning', *Trends in Cognitive Sciences*, 8 (6) (2004): 255–60. The piggy-bank experiment is from Daniela O'Neill, Janet Wilde Astington, and John Flavell's 'Young Children's Understanding of the Role that Sensory Experiences Play in Knowledge Acquisition', *Child Development*, 63 (1992): 474–90. The stock-trading game is from Colin Camerer, George Loewenstein, and Martin Weber's 'The curse of knowledge in economic settings: An experimental analysis', *The Journal of Political Economy*, 97 (5) (1989): 1232–54. The gambler experiment is from Jonathan Baron and John Hershey's 'Outcome bias in decision evaluation', *Journal of Personality and Social Psychology*, 54 (4) (1988): 569–79.

The impact of egocentrism on the intuitions motivating contextualism is explored in Jennifer Nagel's 'Knowledge Ascriptions and the Psychological Consequences of Thinking about Error', *Philosophical Quarterly*, 60 (239) (2010): 286–306.

The first major paper in experimental philosophy is Jonathan Weinberg, Shaun Nichols, and Stephen Stich's 'Normativity and Epistemic Intuitions', *Philosophical Topics*, 29 (2001): 429–60. Ernest Sosa criticizes the Weinberg paper in 'A Defense of the Use of Intuitions in Philosophy', in *Stich and his Critics*, Michael Bishop and Dominic Murphy, (eds), (Oxford: Blackwell, 2008), pp. 101–12.

Work documenting a failure to replicate the original Weinberg results includes Jennifer Nagel, Valerie San Juan, and Raymond Mar's 'Lay denial of knowledge for justified true beliefs', *Cognition*, 129 (2013): 652–6; this paper also includes the experimental findings concerning the story about Albert. John Turri also found no significant differences between North American and South Asian

Gettier case responses, in 'A conspicuous art: putting Gettier to the test', *Philosophers' Imprint*, 13 (10) (2013): 1–16.

Work on the universality of developmental stages in the acquisition of the concept of knowledge includes Henry Wellman, David Cross, and Julianne Watson's 'Meta-analysis of theory-of-mind development: the truth about false belief', *Child Development*, 72.3 (2001): 655–84, and David Liu, Henry M. Wellman, Twila Tardif, and Mark Sabbagh's, 'Theory of mind development in Chinese children: a meta-analysis of false-belief understanding across cultures and languages', *Developmental Psychology*, 44.2 (2008): 523–31. For the Chinese performance advantage, see Shali Wu and Boaz Keysar's 'The effect of culture on perspective taking', *Psychological Science*, 18 (7) (2007): 600–6.

Robert Cummins criticizes reliance on intuition in 'Reflection on Reflective Equilibrium', in Michael DePaul and William Ramsey (eds), *Rethinking Intuition: The Psychology of Intuition and Its Role in Philosophical Inquiry* (Oxford: Rowman & Littlefield, 1998), pp. 113–27; the quotation is from p. 124.

References

Further reading

Chapter 1: Introduction

The open-access archive Philpapers (<http://www.philpapers.org>)
  contains thousands of papers in epistemology, including most
  of those referenced here, organized into topic areas and searchable
  by keyword. In some cases the description of a paper links into
  a journal that is accessible only through a paywall (or from a
  computer with a subscription to the journal), but many of the papers
  are archived within Philpapers itself and are freely accessible.

There is a good discussion of group knowledge attributions in
  Alexander Bird's 'Social Knowing', *Philosophical Perspectives*,
  24 (1) (2010): 23–56. For a clear survey of work on the relationship
  between individual and group judgement see Fabrizio Cariani's
  'Judgment Aggregation', *Philosophy Compass*, 6 (2011): 22–32.

For a thorough examination of Protagoras's relativism, and Plato's
  response to it, see Myles Burnyeat's edition of Plato's *Theaetetus*
  (Indianapolis: Hackett, 1990) which includes a detailed and
  helpful introduction.

For a contemporary defence of relativism, see John MacFarlane's entry
  on relativism in *The Routledge Companion to the Philosophy of
  Language* (New York: Routledge, 2012).

Chapter 2: Scepticism

Charles Brittain's collection *On Academic Scepticism* contains the core
  texts and a useful introduction (Indianapolis: Hackett Publishing
  Company, 2006).

The lives and main ideas of ancient Greek sceptics are well covered in the *Stanford Encyclopedia of Philosophy* (online at <http://plato.stanford.edu/>).

One of the few positive contemporary defences of scepticism is Peter Unger's book, *Ignorance: A Case for Skepticism* (New York: Oxford University Press, 1975). Barry Stroud's *The Significance of Philosophical Scepticism* (New York: Oxford University Press, 1984) doesn't advocate scepticism, but Stroud takes the Dreaming Argument very seriously, and argues that there is still no fully satisfactory response to it.

Readers interested in Indian scepticism will enjoy Chapter two of Bimal Matital's book *Perception: An Essay on Classical Indian Theories of Knowledge* (Oxford: Oxford University Press, 1986).

Moore's position on the sceptical problem is now sometimes known as 'dogmatism'. For a revival of the Moorean way of looking at things, see James Pryor's 'The Skeptic and the Dogmatist', *Noûs*, 34 (4) (2000): 517–49.

Chapter 3: Rationalism and empiricism

Michael Matthew's collection *The Scientific Background to Modern Philosophy* (Indianapolis: Hackett, 1989) includes a wide range of interesting selections from scientists working in and just before the Early Modern period.

Gary Hatfield's *Stanford Encyclopedia of Philosophy* entry on Descartes (<http://plato.stanford.edu/entries/descartes/>) provides a good overview, as does Tom Sorrell's *Descartes: A Very Short Introduction* (Oxford: Oxford University Press, 2001). For more philosophical detail, readers can consult the essays in Janet Broughton and John Carreiro's *A Companion to Descartes* (Malden, MA: Blackwell, 2008). Readers interested in the life of Descartes will enjoy Stephen Gaukroger's *Descartes: An Intellectual Biography* (New York: Oxford University Press, 1995).

Descartes's *Meditations* were published with a series of objections by Descartes's contemporaries (including the prominent French theologian Antoine Arnauld and the prominent English philosopher Hobbes), together with Descartes's replies. These are freely available online, and in most full published editions of the *Meditations*. Descartes's correspondence with Elizabeth was not published in his day, but is now available in a translation by Lisa

Shapiro: *The Correspondence Between Princess Elizabeth of Bohemia and René Descartes* (Chicago: University of Chicago Press, 2007).

On Locke, after starting with the *Stanford Encyclopedia* entry by William Uzgalis (<http://plato.stanford.edu/entries/locke/>), readers can consult the *Cambridge Companion to Locke* (Cambridge: Cambridge University Press, 1994), and for more detail on the theory of knowledge, the *Cambridge Companion to Locke's Essay Concerning Human Understanding* (Cambridge: Cambridge University Press, 2007). Roger Woolhouse's *Locke: A Biography* (Cambridge: Cambridge University Press, 2007) is also recommended reading.

Chapter 4: The analysis of knowledge

Robert Shope's book *The Analysis of Knowing: A Decade of Research* (Princeton: Princeton University Press, 1983) is a great survey of all the early fights over Gettier's definition of knowledge.

More recent work is well covered in the *Stanford Encyclopedia of Philosophy* entry on the analysis of knowledge, by Jonathan Jenkins Ichikawa and Matthew Steup (<http://plato.stanford.edu/entries/knowledge-analysis/>).

Chapter 5: Internalism and externalism

Hilary Kornblith's collection *Epistemology: Internalism and Externalism* (Malden, MA: Wiley-Blackwell, 2001) is a good selection of the core early writings on either side of the internalism–externalism controversy.

The classic statement of 20th century internalism is Roderick Chisholm's *Theory of Knowledge* (Englewood Cliffs, NJ: Prentice-Hall, 1966).

Externalism is defended in Alvin Goldman's *Epistemology and Cognition* (Cambridge, MA: Harvard University Press, 1986) and in Timothy Williamson's *Knowledge and its Limits* (Oxford: Oxford University Press, 2000).

For a clear summary of the internalism–externalism controversy, see James Pryor's 2001 paper 'Highlights of Recent Epistemology', *British Journal for the Philosophy of Science*, 52: 95–124.

Chapter 6: Testimony

For a concise introduction to reductionism and non-reductionism, see
Jennifer Lackey's 'Knowing from Testimony', *Philosophy Compass*,
1:5 (2006): 432–48. Jennifer Lackey and Ernest Sosa's edited
collection *The Epistemology of Testimony* contains essays
representing a broad spectrum of philosophical perspectives on
testimony (Oxford: Oxford University Press, 2006).

For more on the classical Indian line on testimony, see Stephen Phillips's
Stanford Encyclopedia entry on Classical Indian Epistemology:
<http://plato.stanford.edu/entries/epistemology-india/>.

Chapter 7: Shifting standards?

Patrick Rysiew's *Stanford Encyclopedia of Philosophy* entry on
contextualism is an excellent overview of the position: <http://plato.
stanford.edu/entries/contextualism-epistemology/>.

For a collection of influential essays for and against contextualism, see
Contextualism in Philosophy: Knowledge, Meaning and Truth,
Gerhard Preyer and Georg Peter (eds) (New York: Oxford
University Press, 2005).

Chapter 8: Knowing about knowing

For an overview of empirical work on mindreading, see Ian Apperly's
Mindreaders: The Cognitive Basis of 'Theory of Mind' (Hove:
Psychology Press, 2011).

For various perspectives on experimental philosophy, see *Current
Controversies in Experimental Philosophy*, Edouard Machery and
Elizabeth O'Neill (eds) (New York: Routledge, 2014).

There are interesting discussions of the role of intuitions in philosophy
in Hilary Kornblith's *Knowledge and its Place in Nature* (Oxford:
Oxford University Press, 2005), in Timothy Williamson's *The
Philosophy of Philosophy* (Oxford: Oxford University Press, 2007),
and in Tamar Szabó Gendler's *Intuition, Imagination, and
Philosophical Methodology* (Oxford University Press, 2010).

Index

Index

SOCIAL MEDIA
Very Short Introduction

Join our community
www.oup.com/vsi

- Join us online at the official Very Short Introductions **Facebook** page.
- Access the thoughts and musings of our authors with our online **blog**.
- Sign up for our monthly **e-newsletter** to receive information on all new titles publishing that month.
- Browse the full range of Very Short Introductions online.
- Read **extracts** from the Introductions for free.
- Visit our library of **Reading Guides**. These guides, written by our expert authors will help you to question again, why you think what you think.
- If you are a teacher or lecturer you can order inspection copies quickly and simply via our website.